Just Put An Eye On It!

by

Georgevine Moss

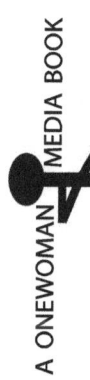

A ONEWOMAN MEDIA BOOK

CONTENTS

PORTRAITS 5

COLOR & PAINT

ILLUSTRATIONS 67

COLOR

AQUARIUM 69   WALL 75   FENCE 77   DEFENCE 85   THE BATS COURT 83

BIRDS 71   STREET 73   THE CHARMS COURT 79   FREE THROW LINE 81

JUST PUT AN EYE ON IT! 89

DRAW

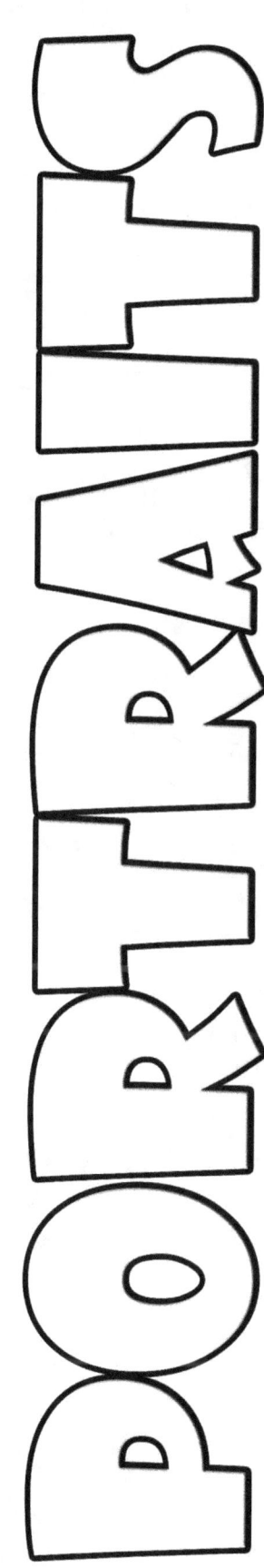

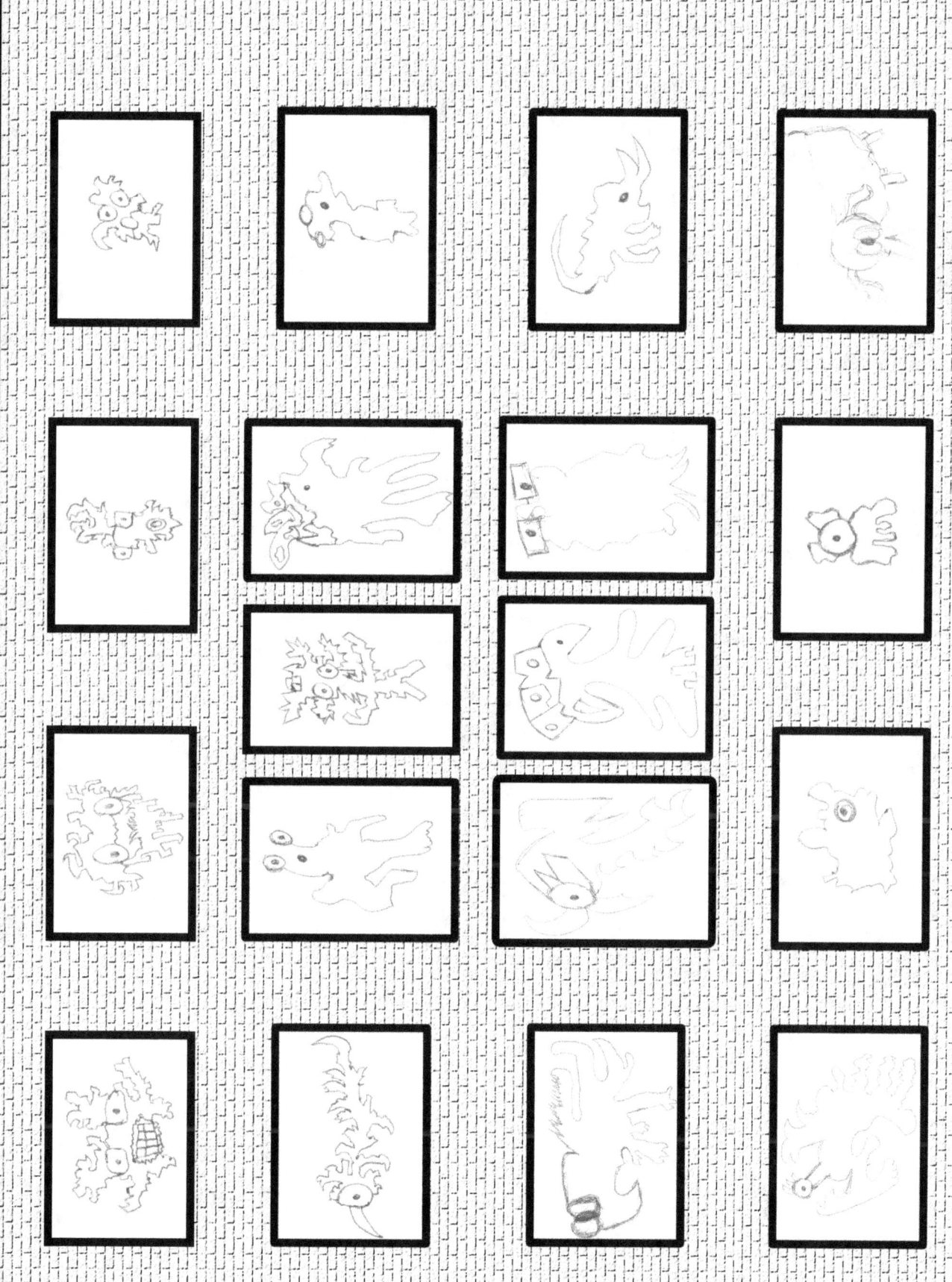

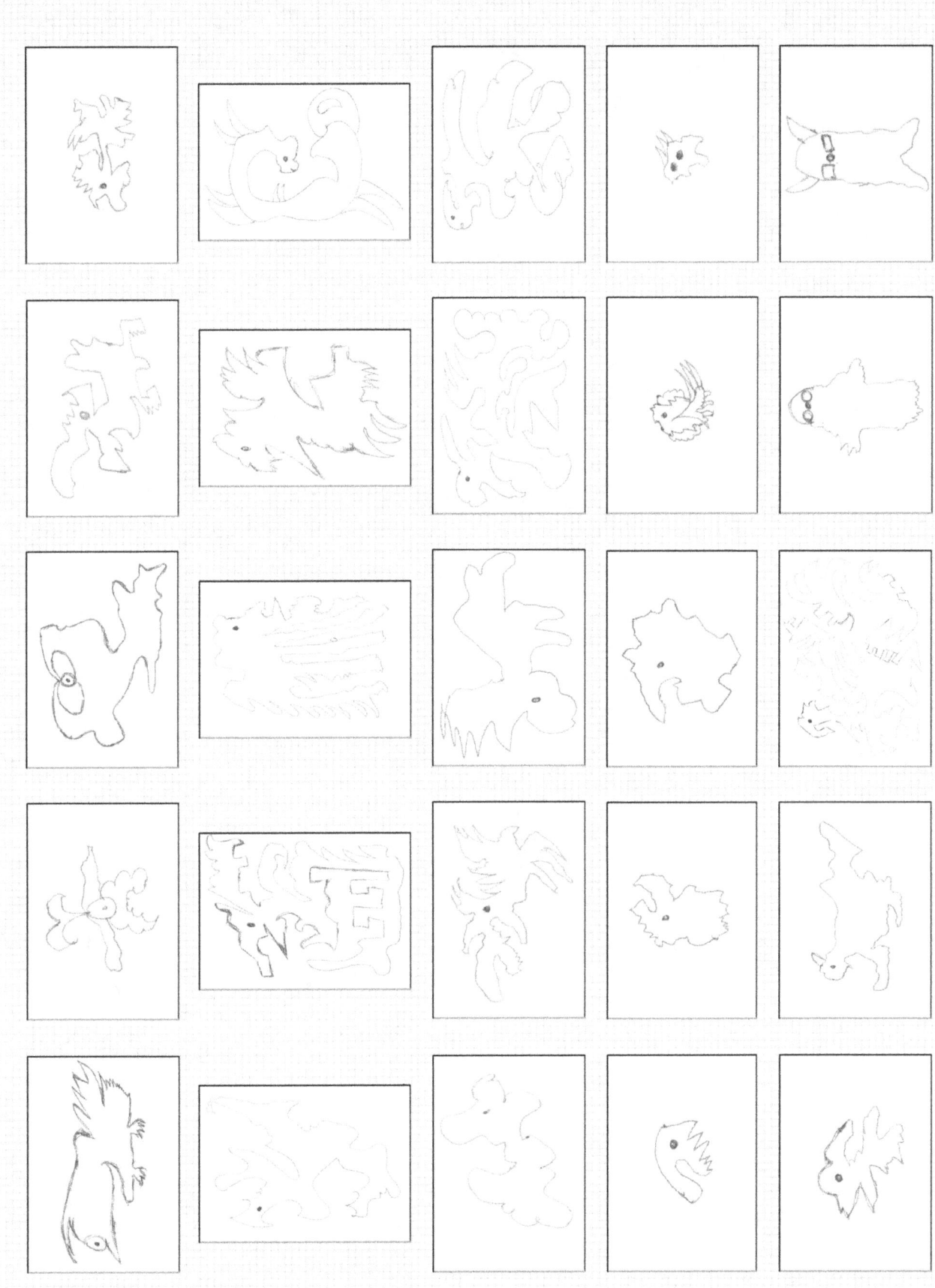

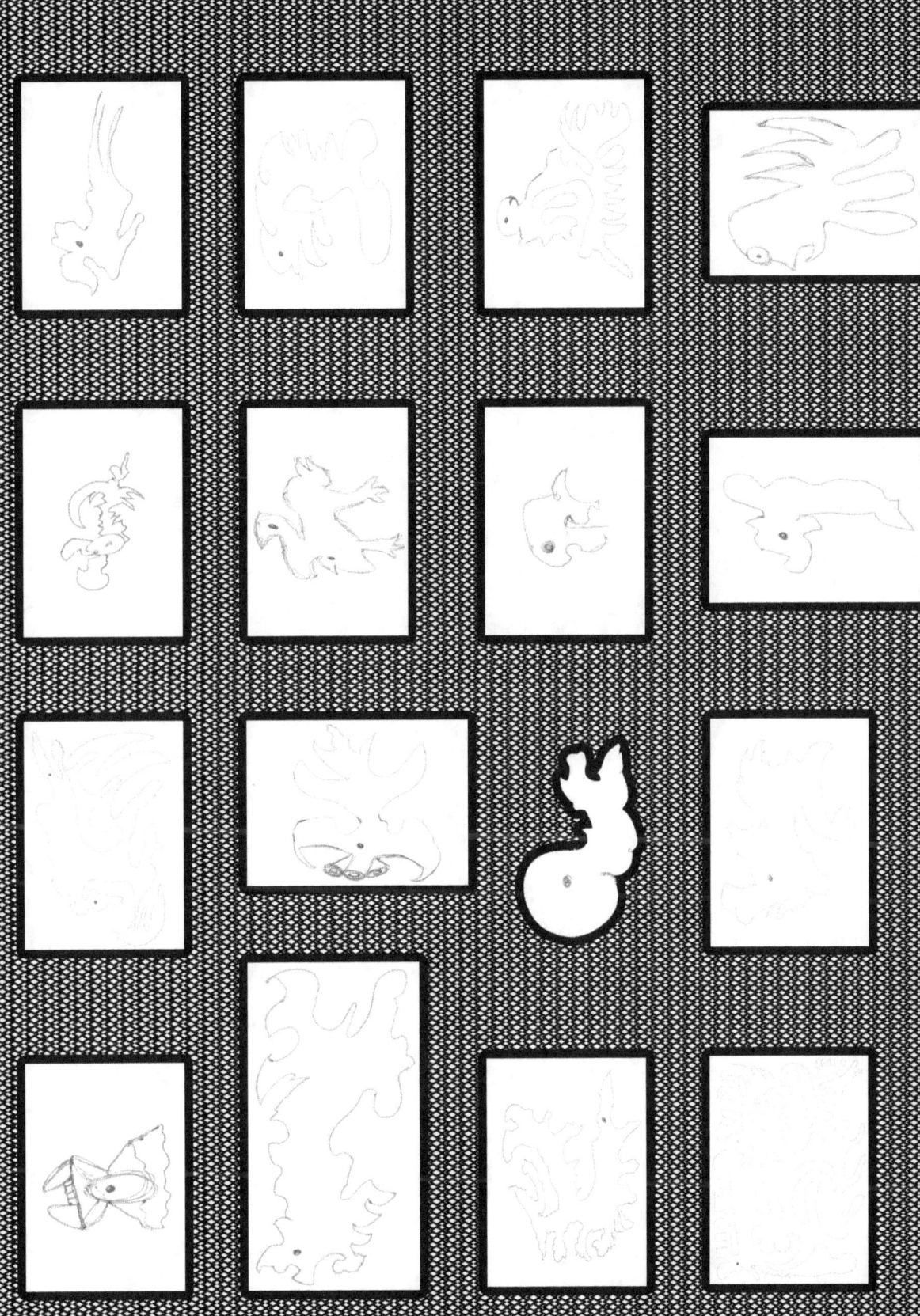

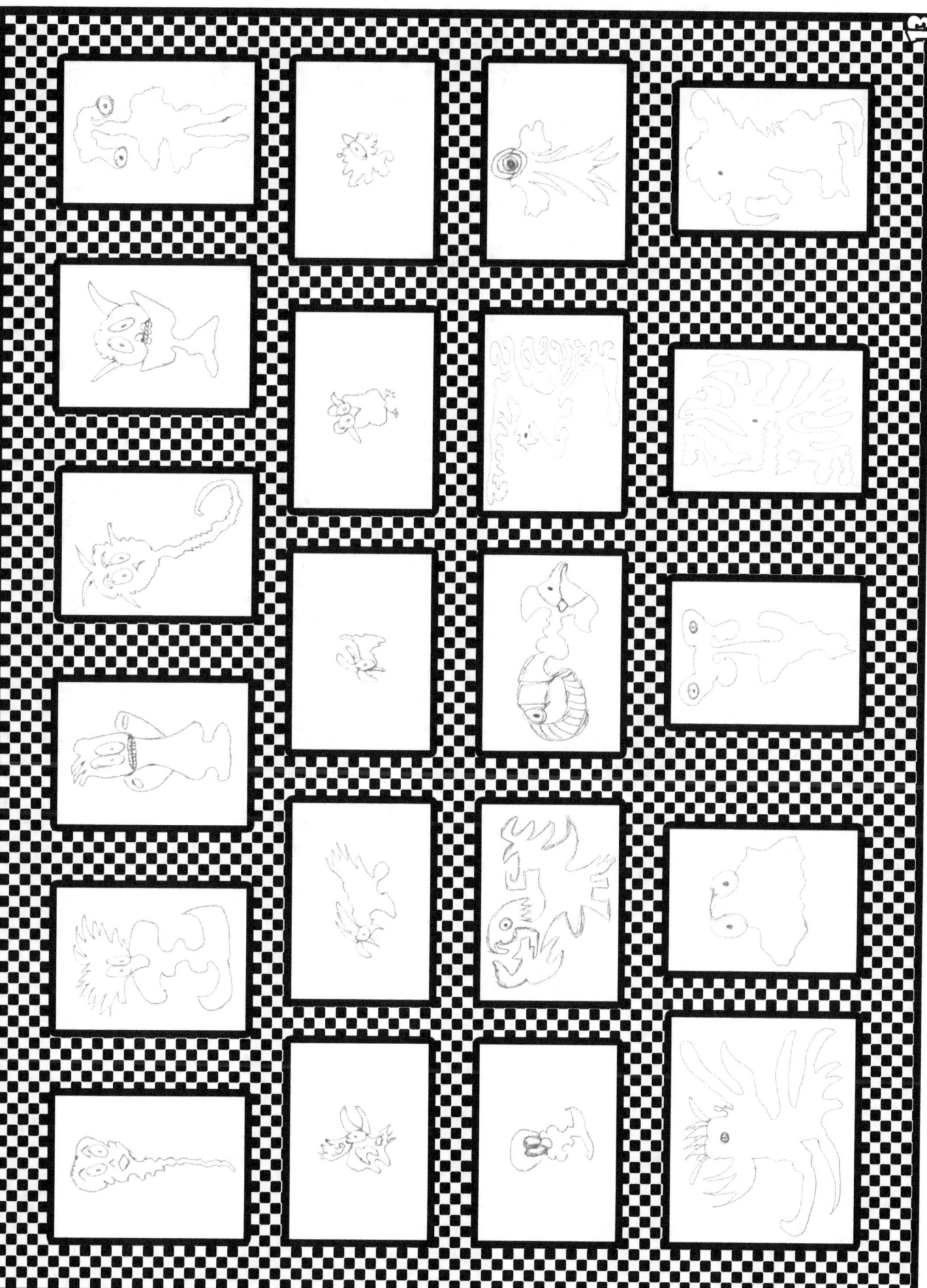

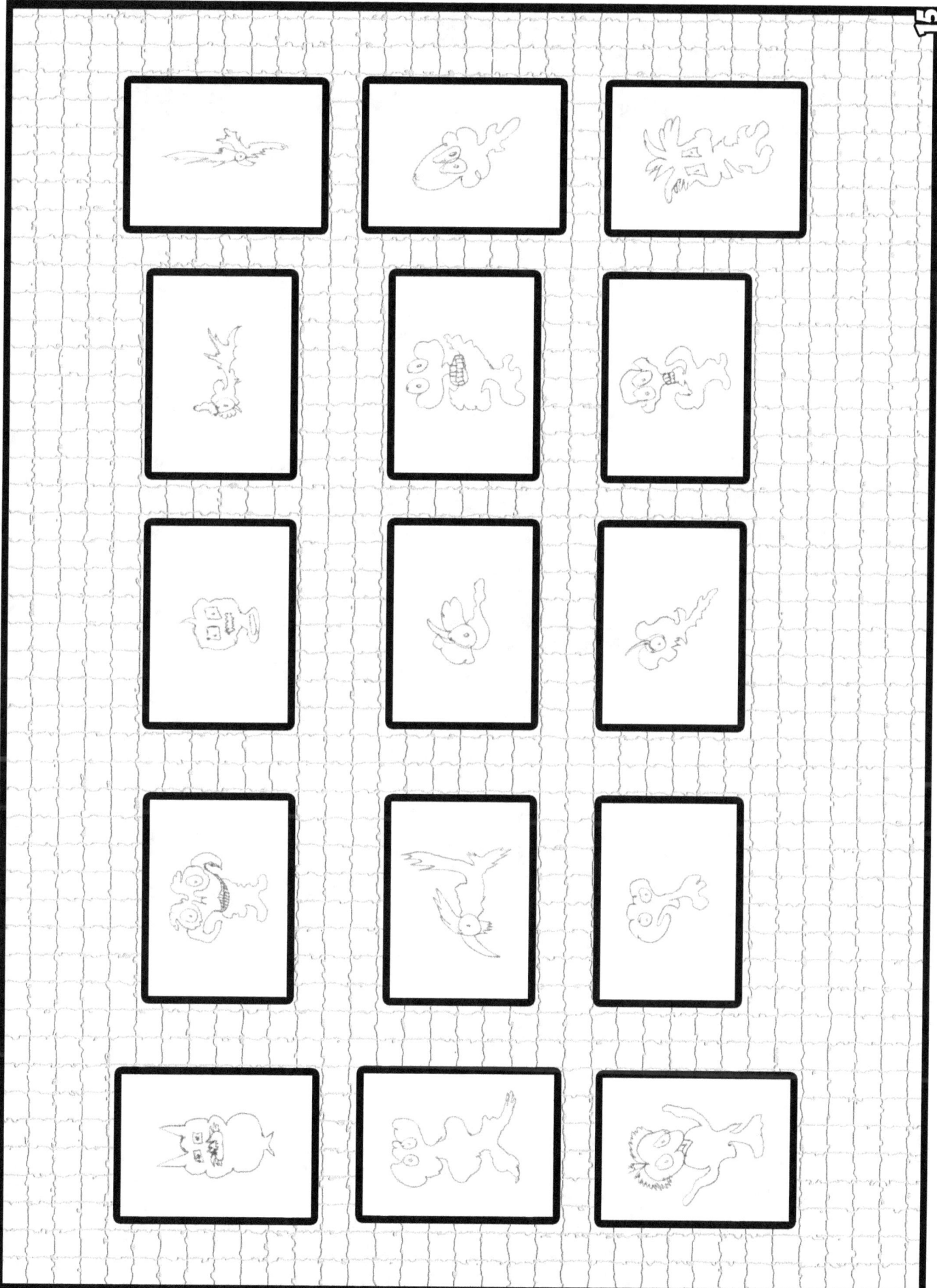

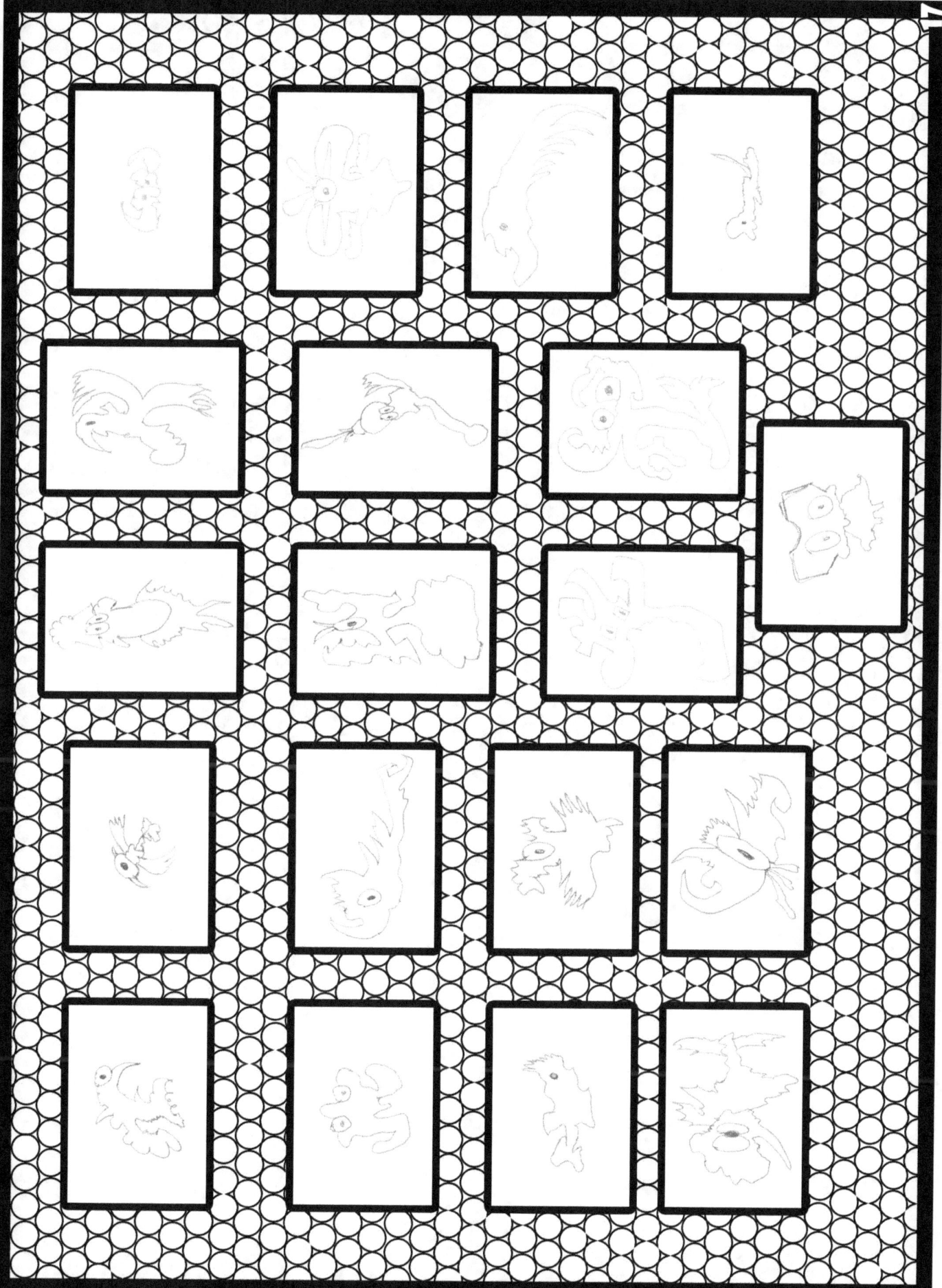

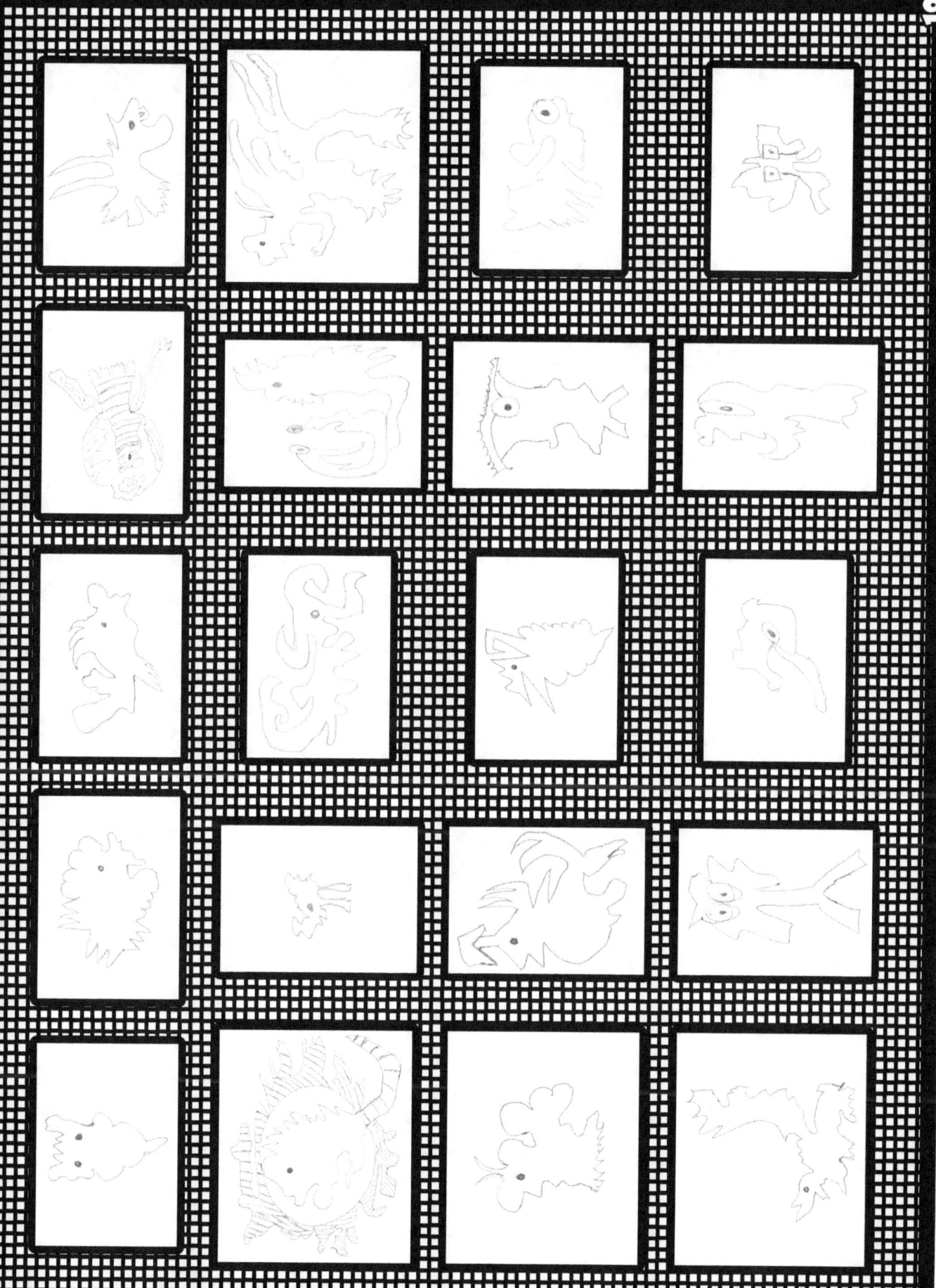

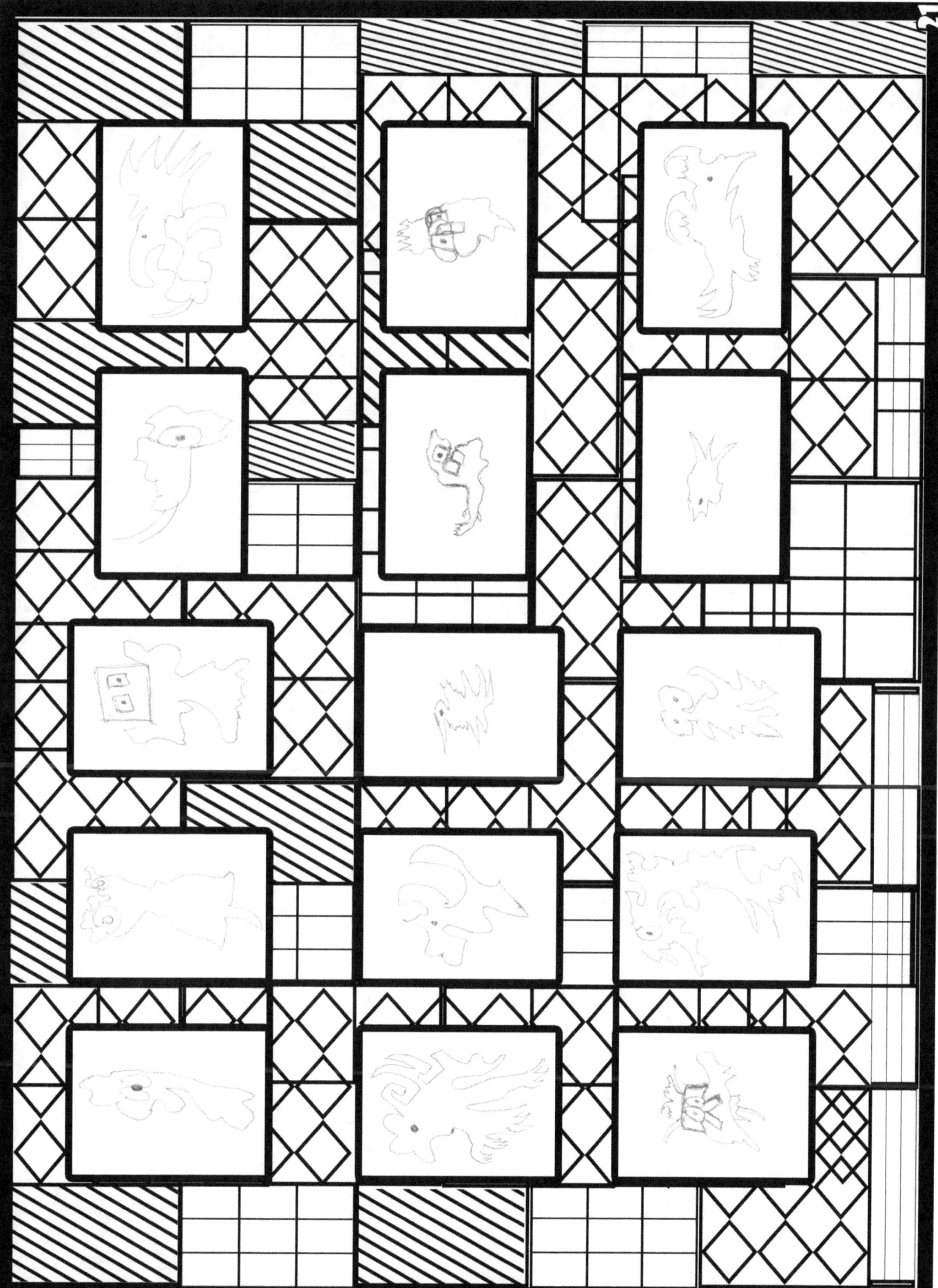

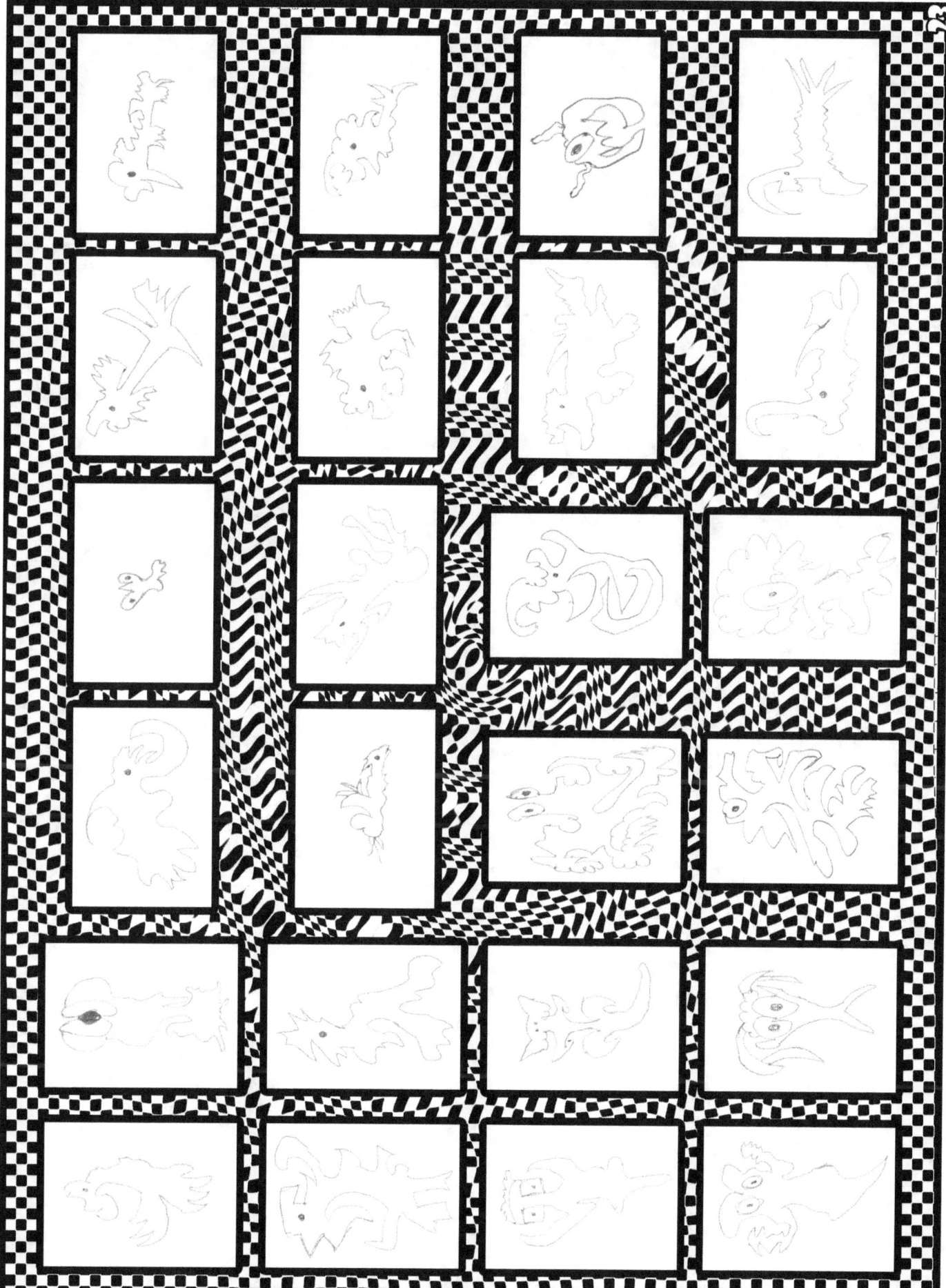

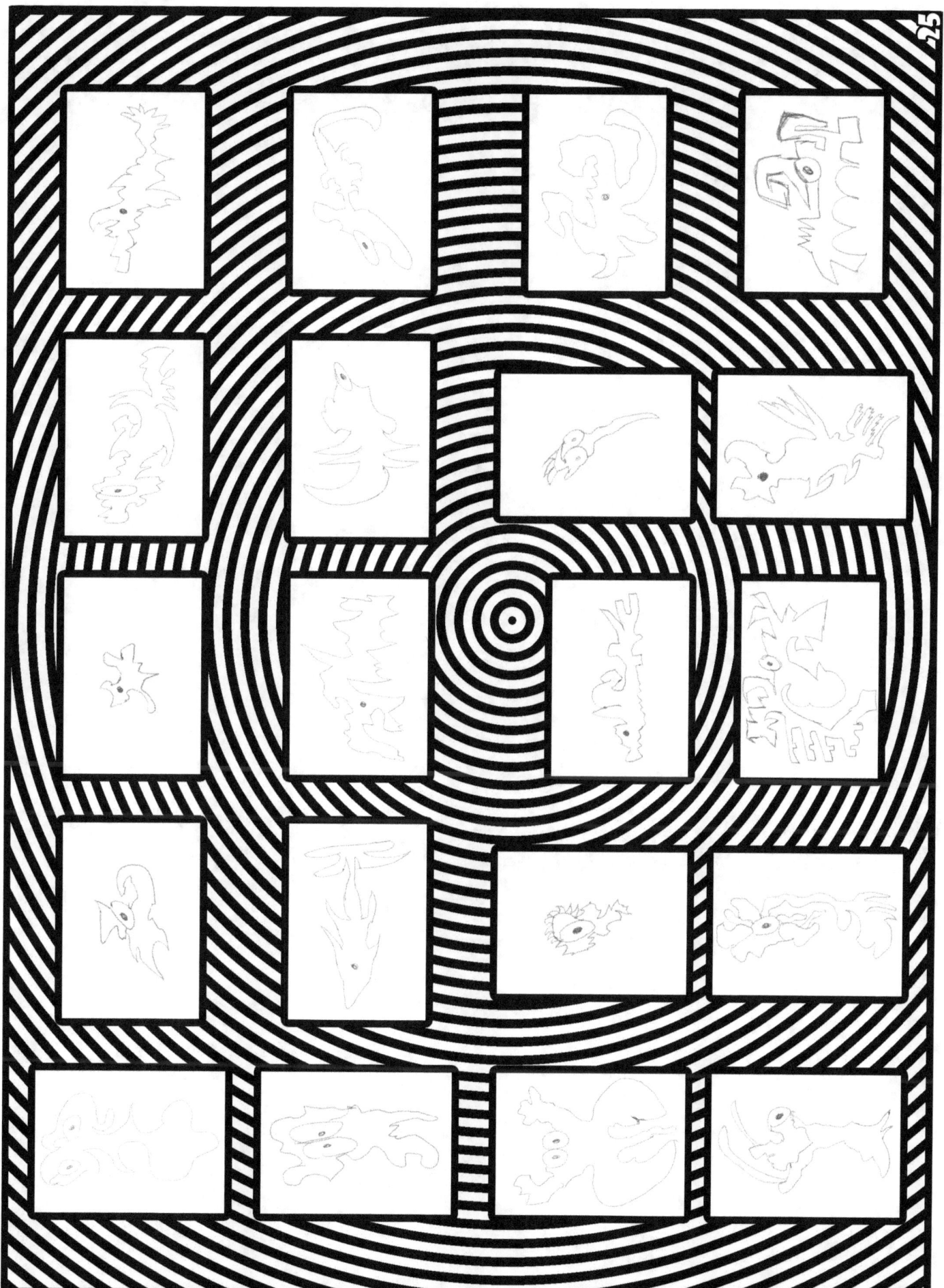

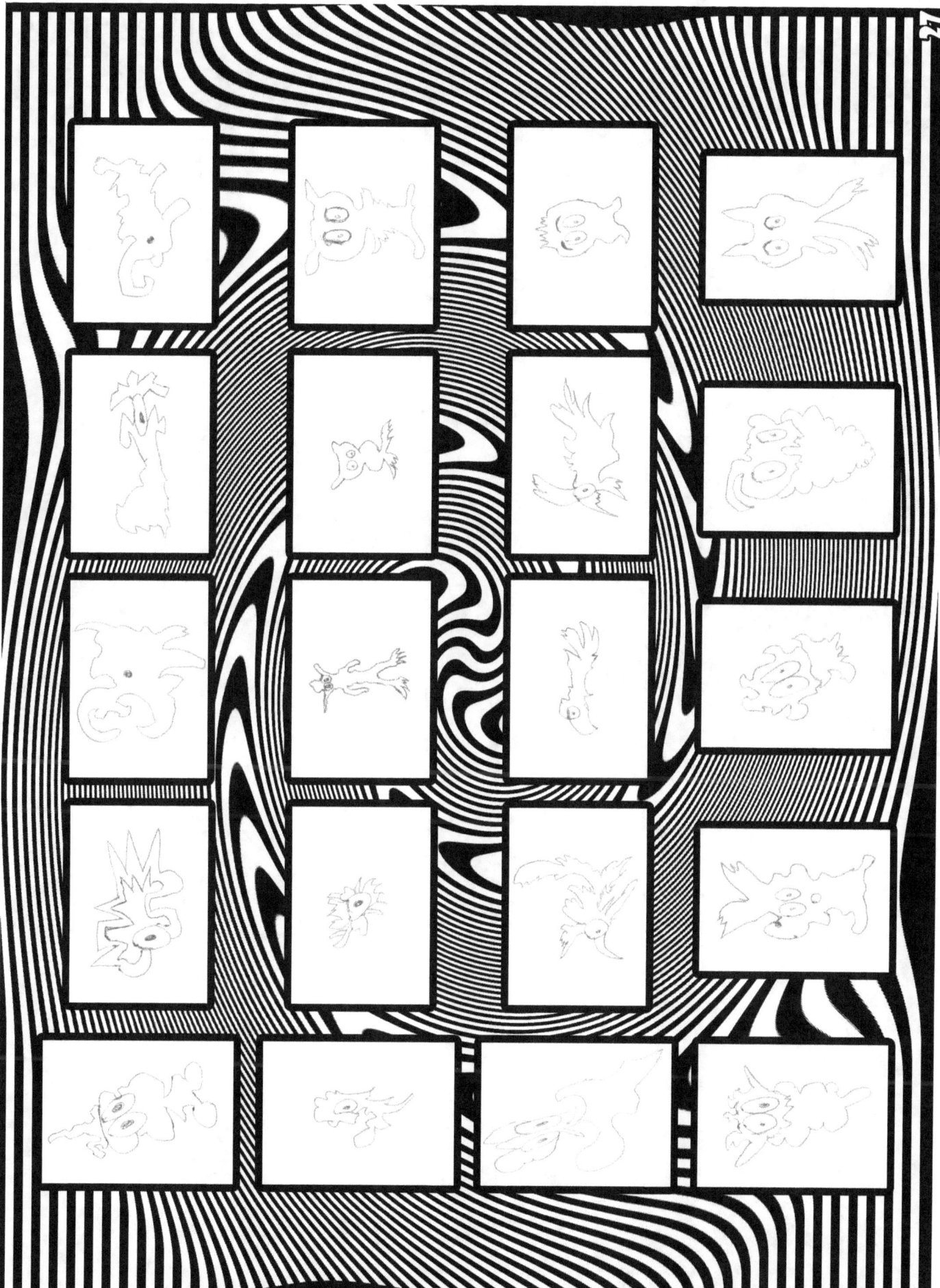

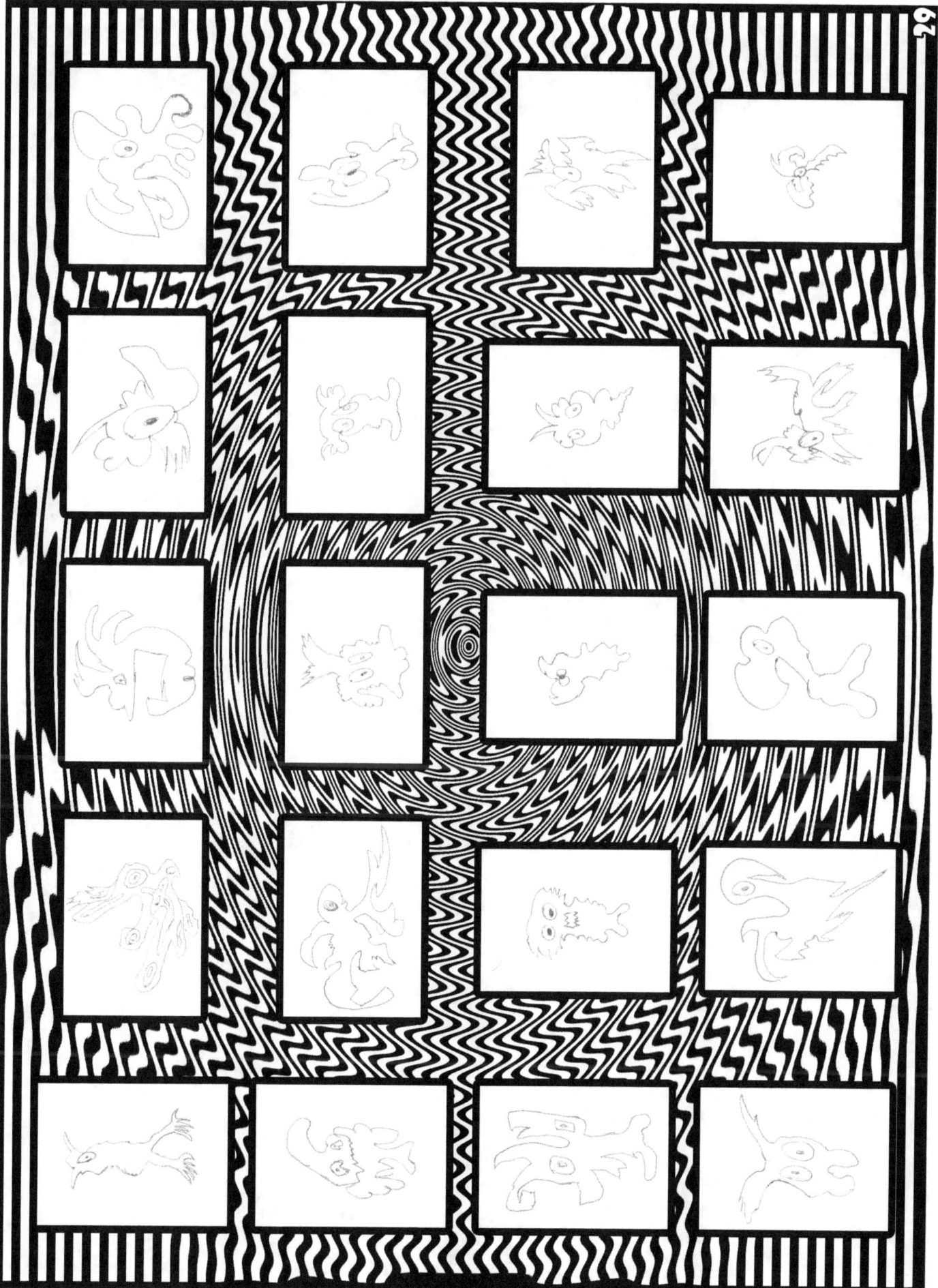

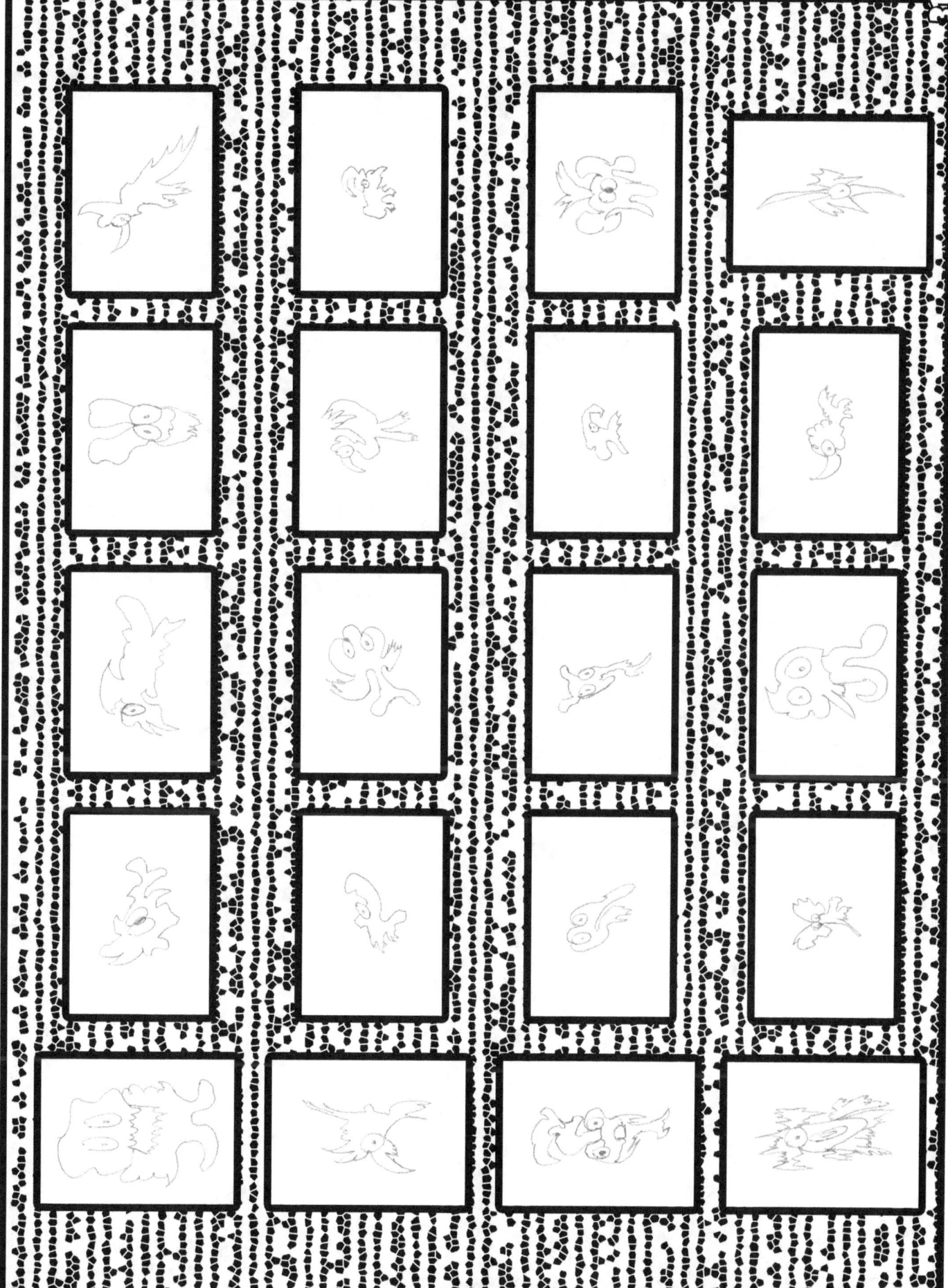

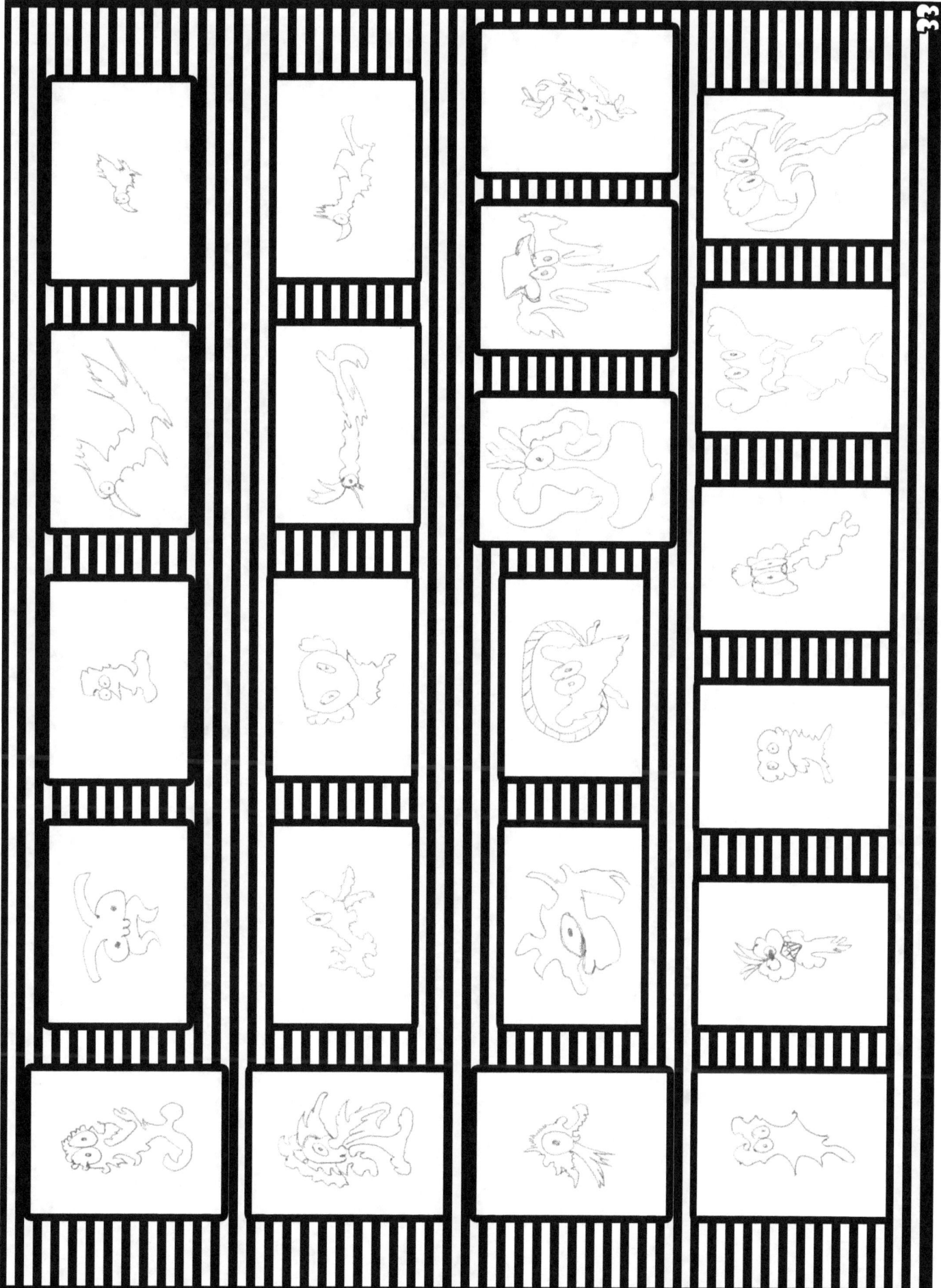

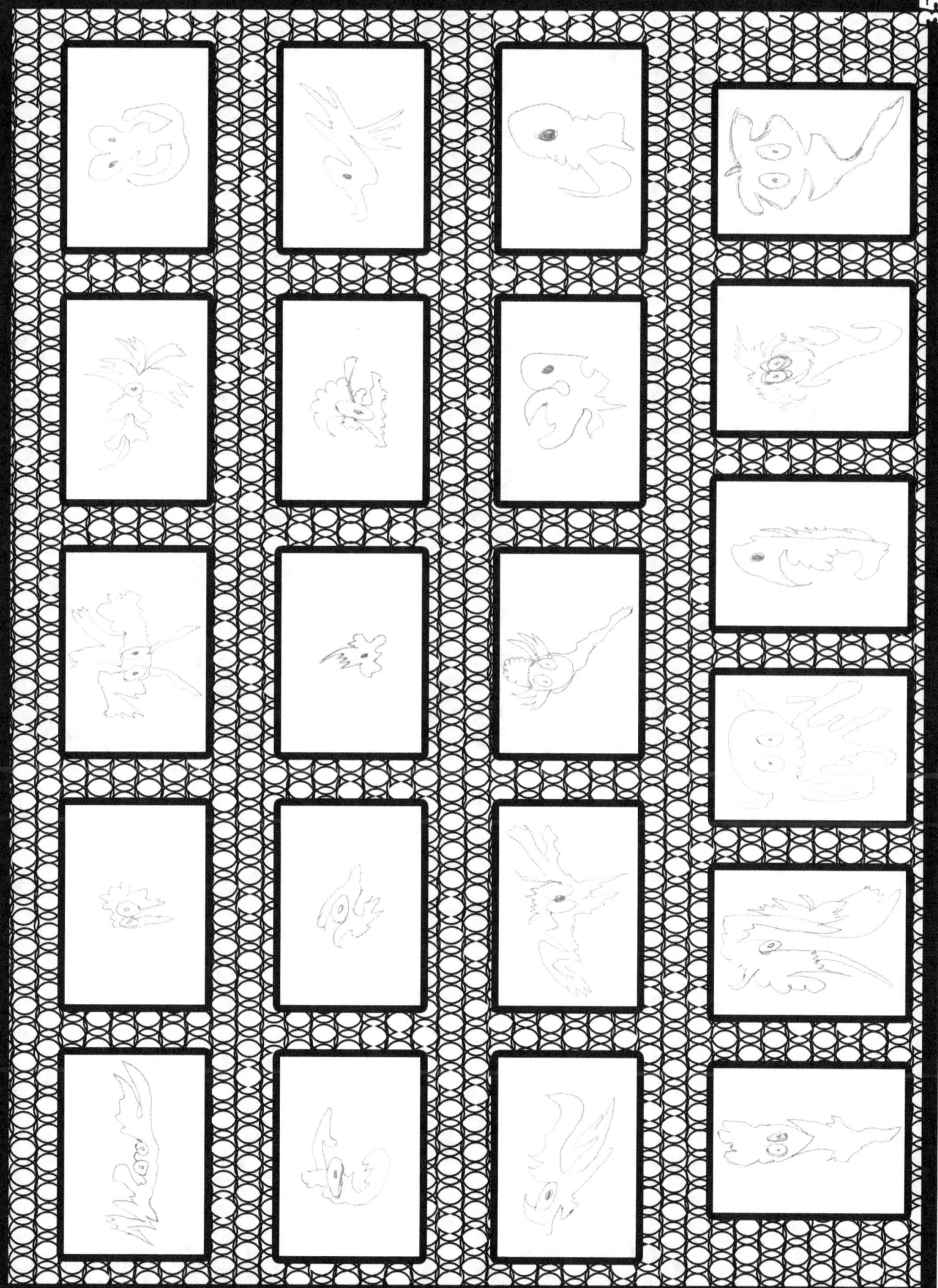

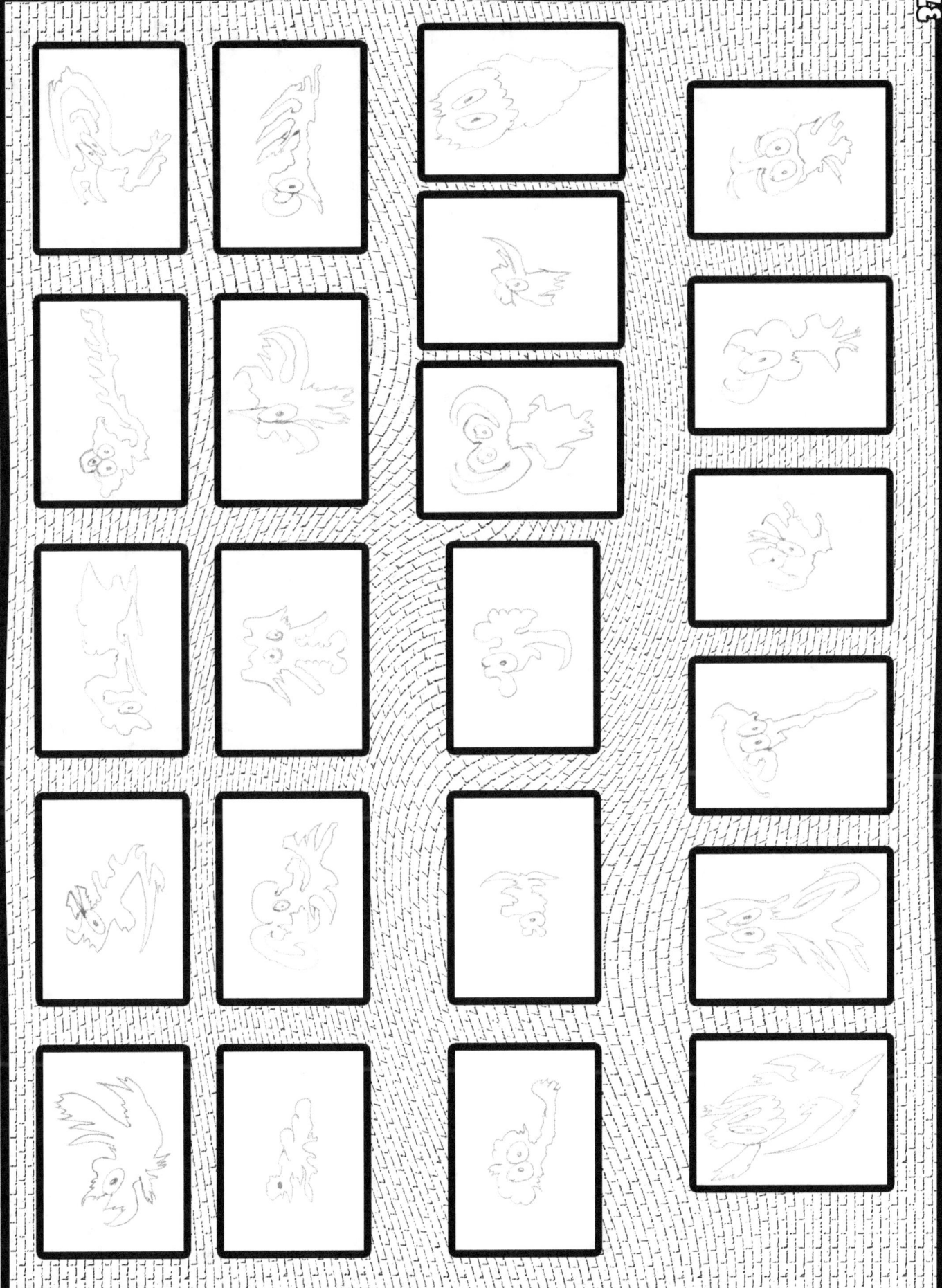

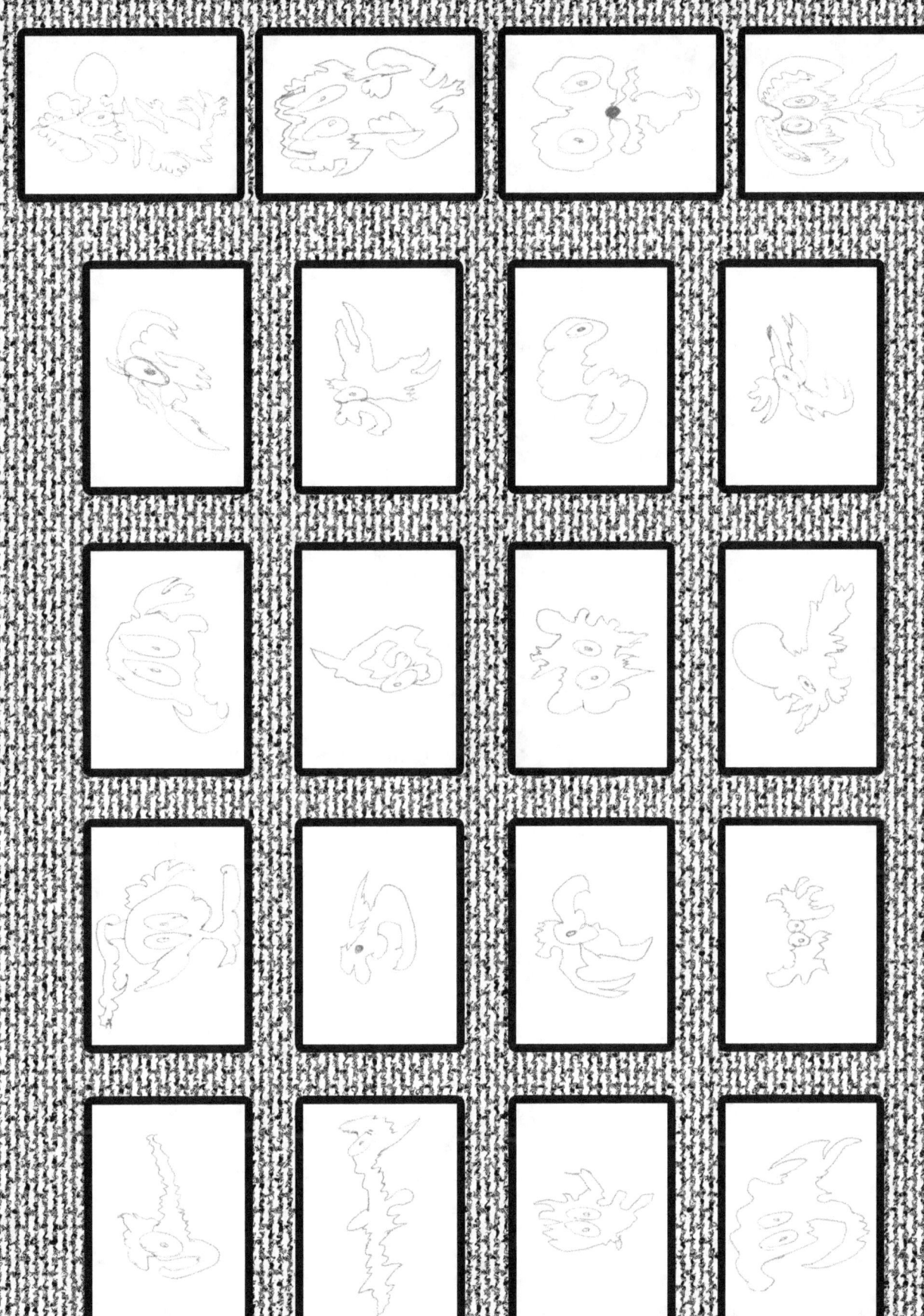

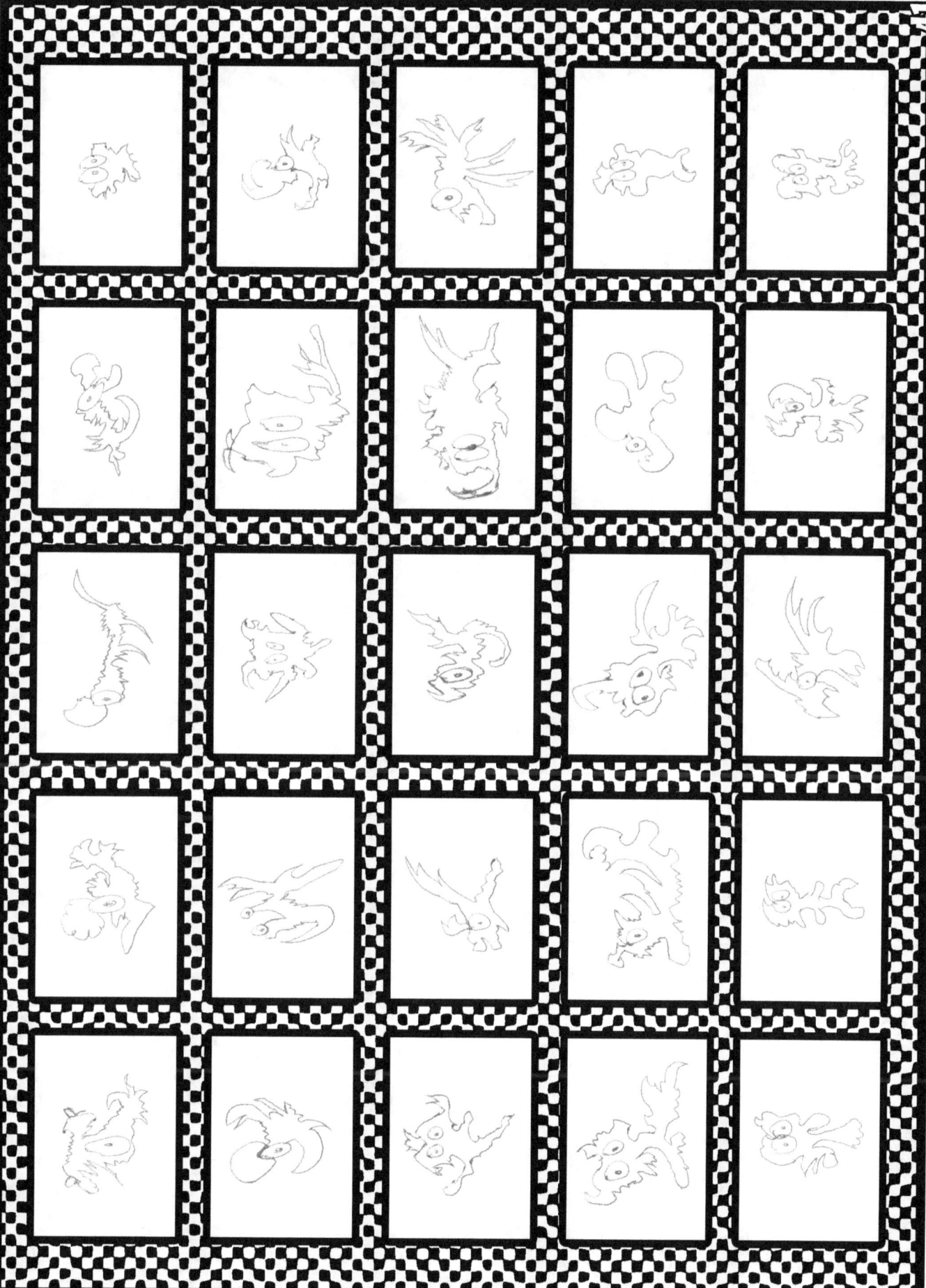

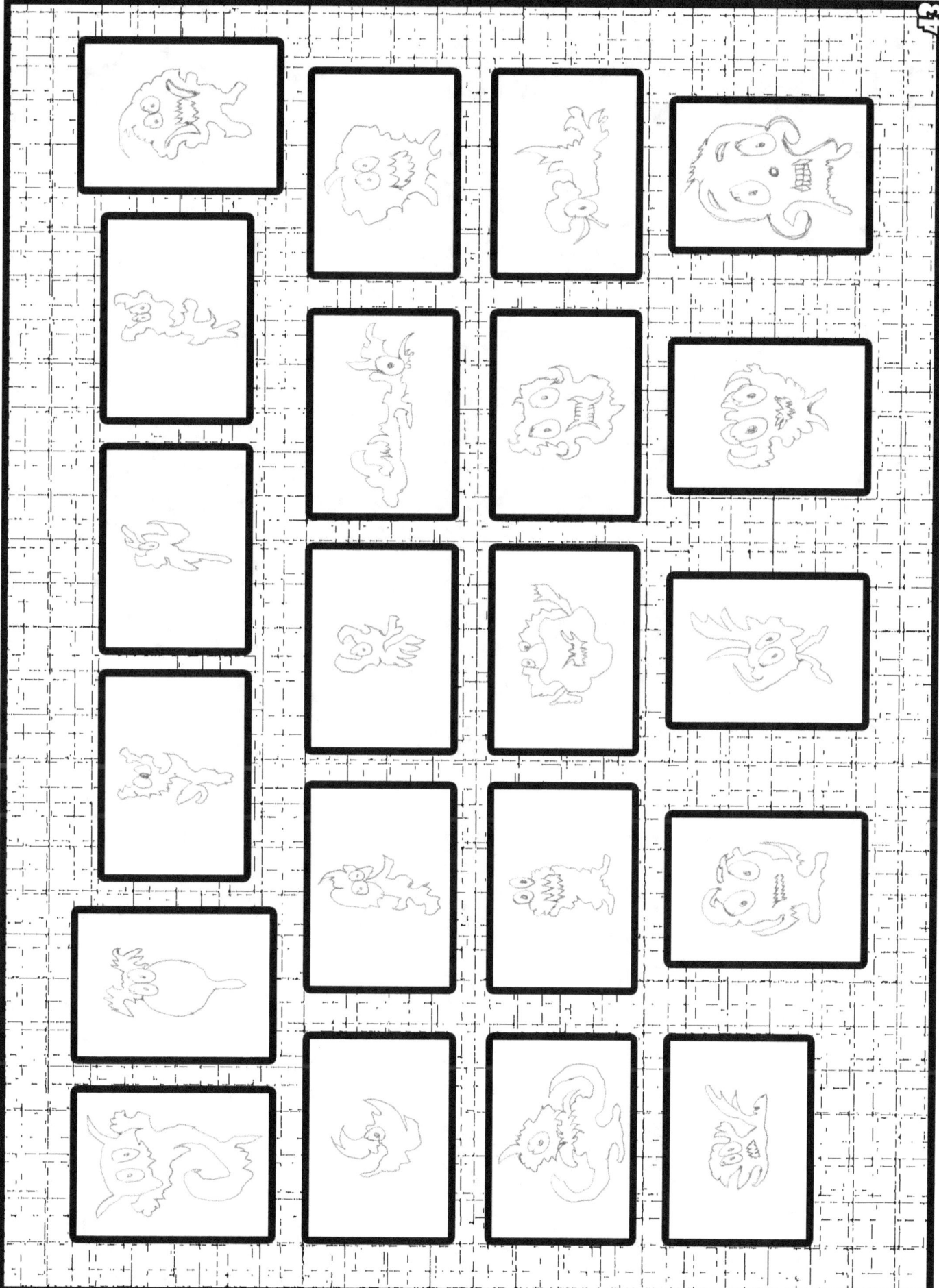

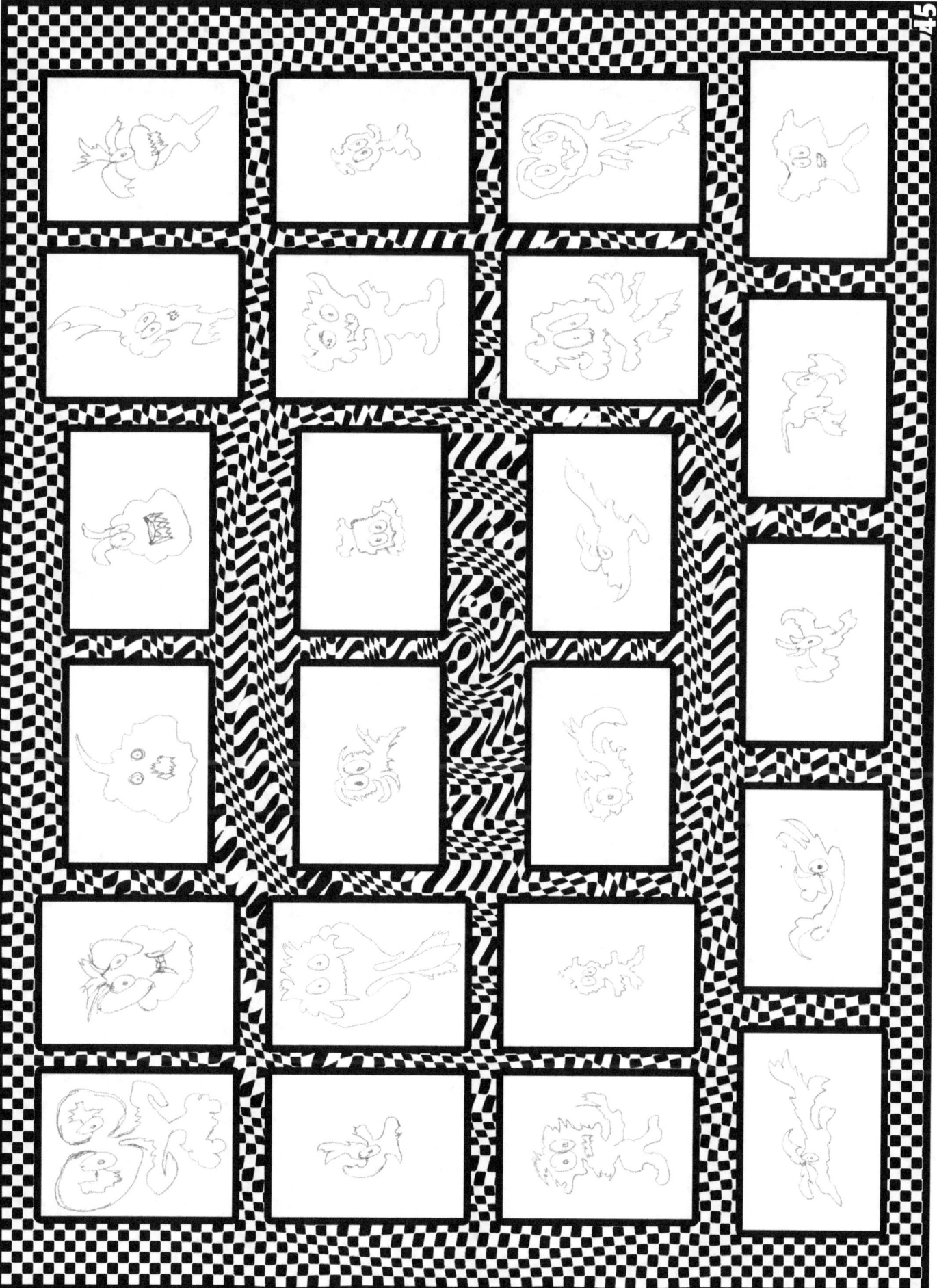

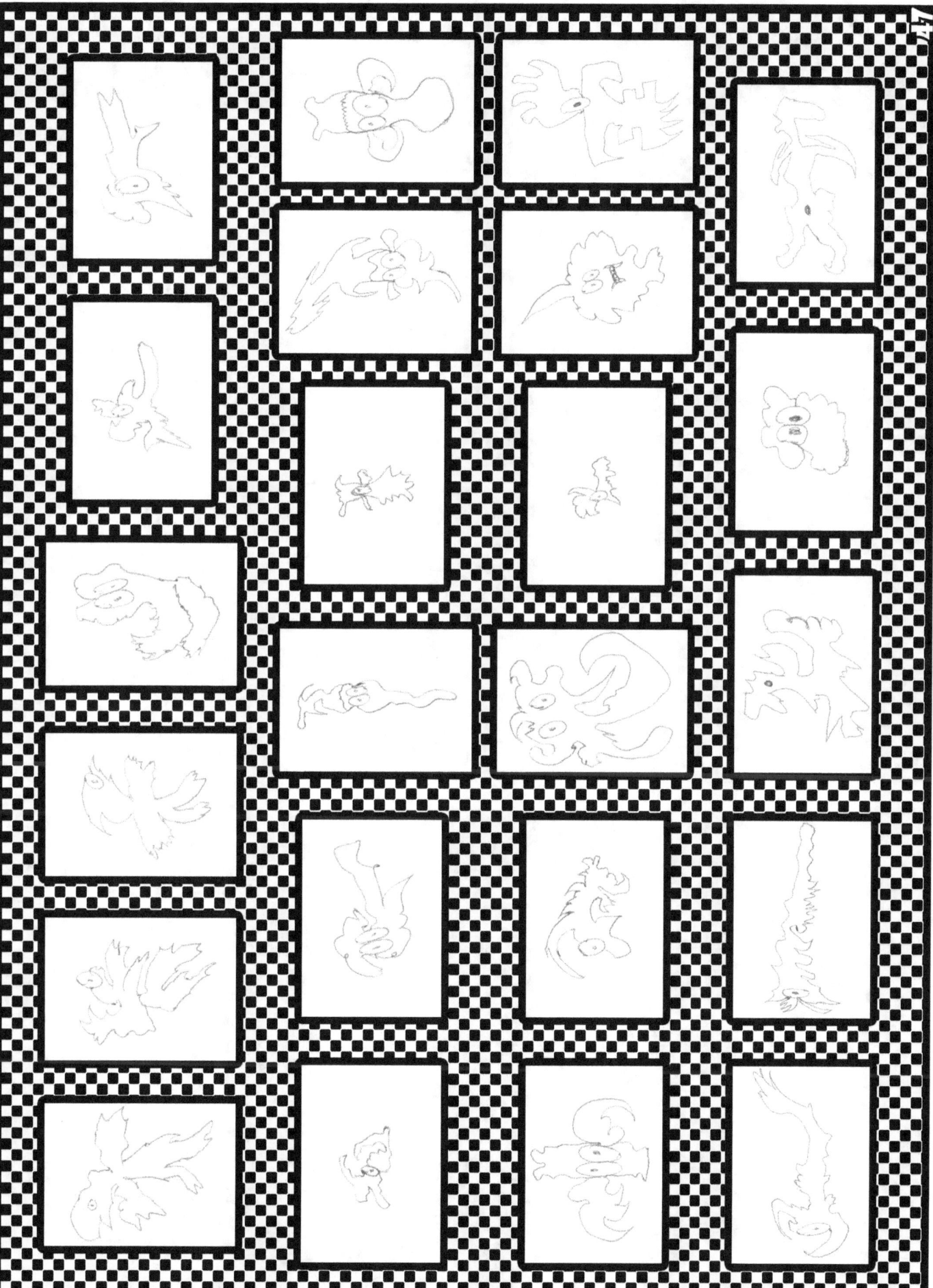

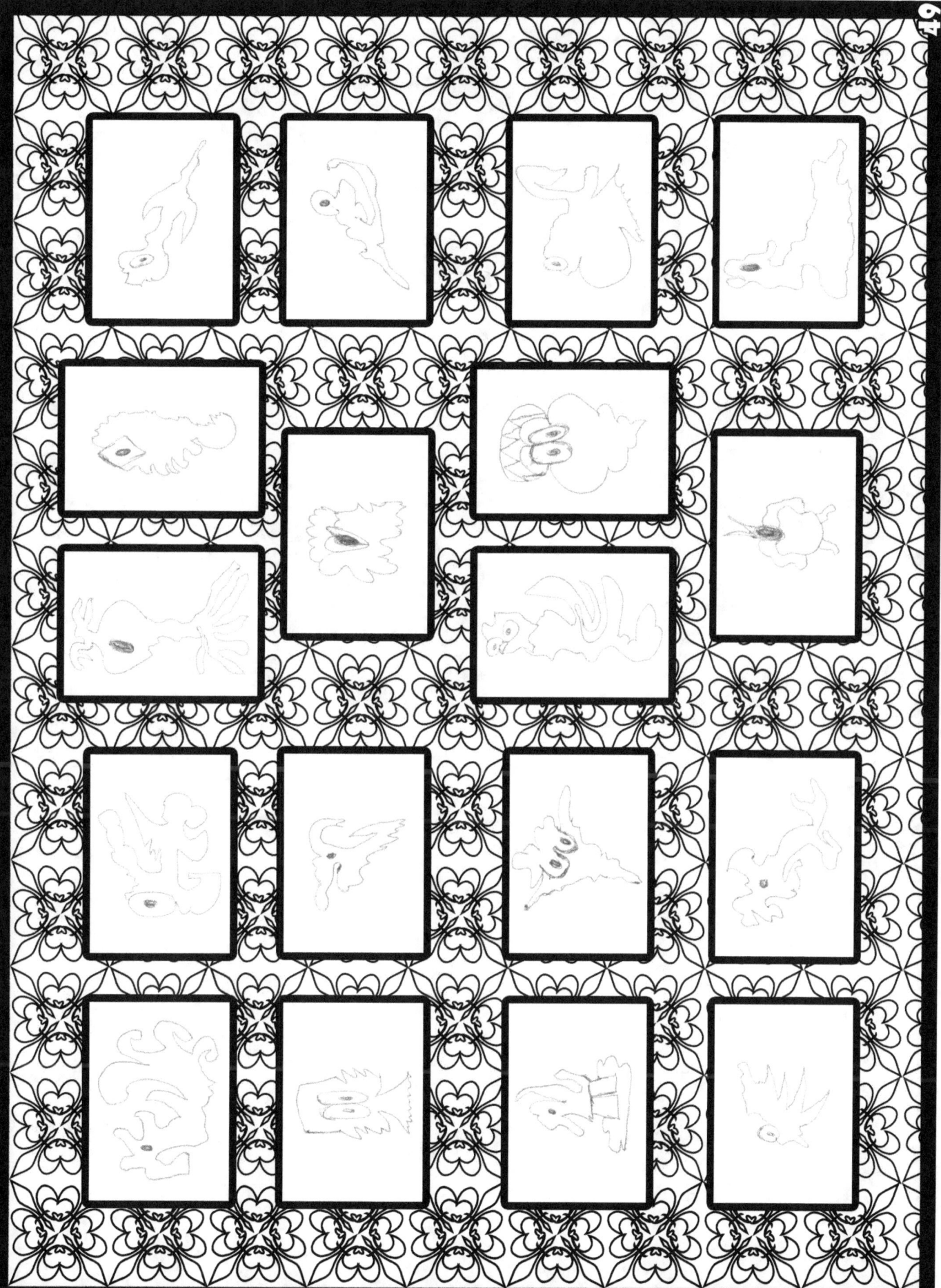

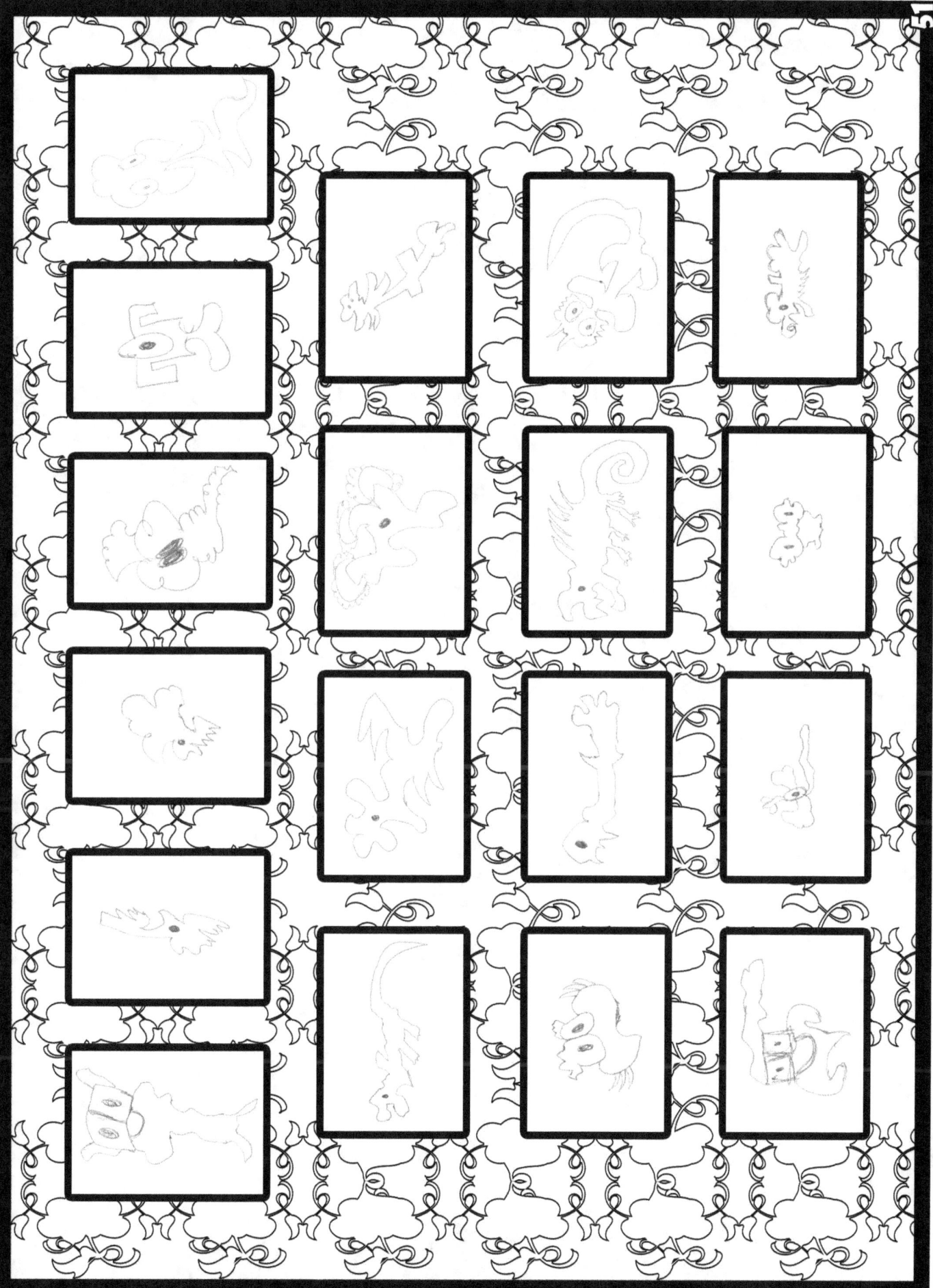

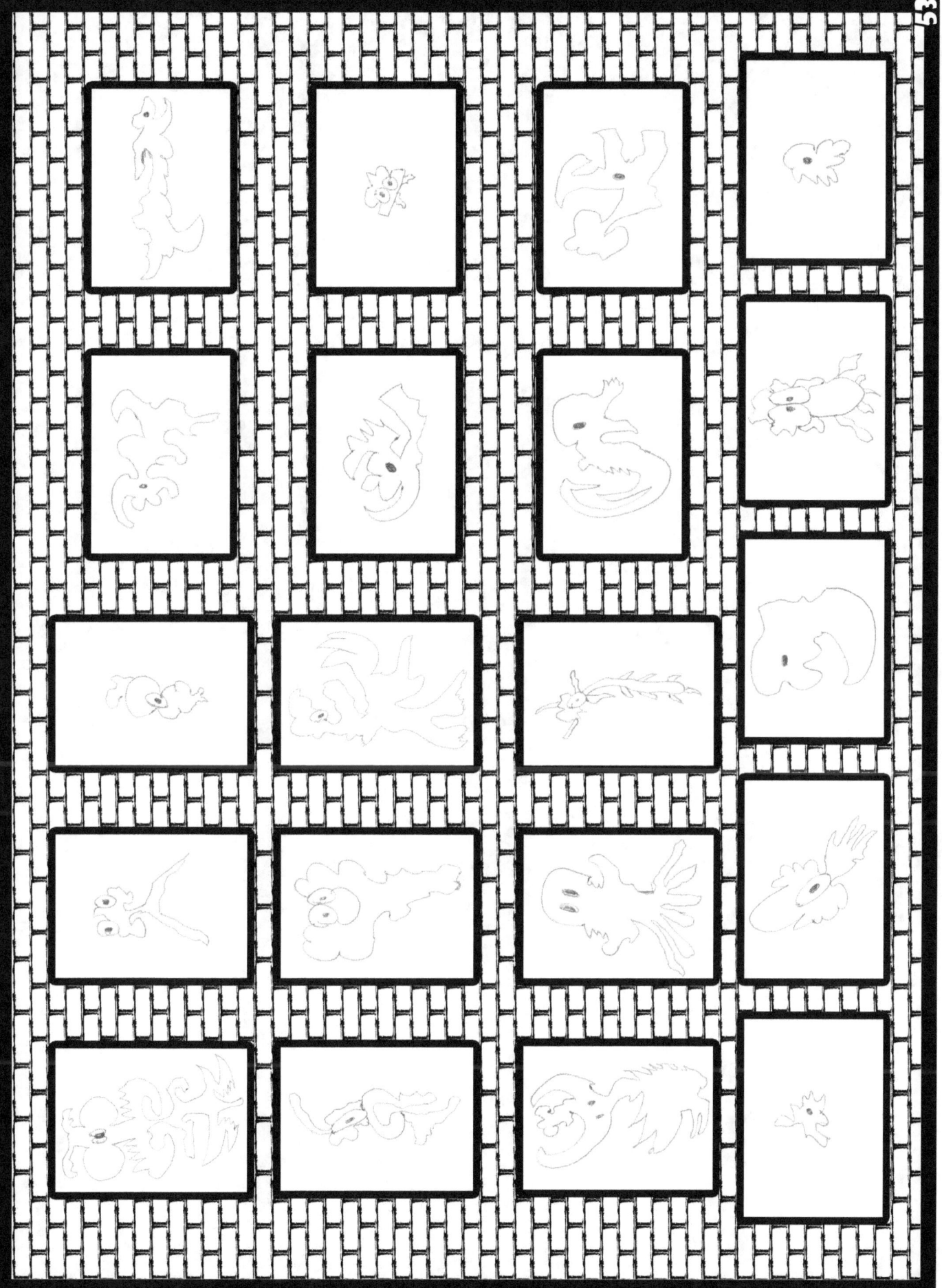

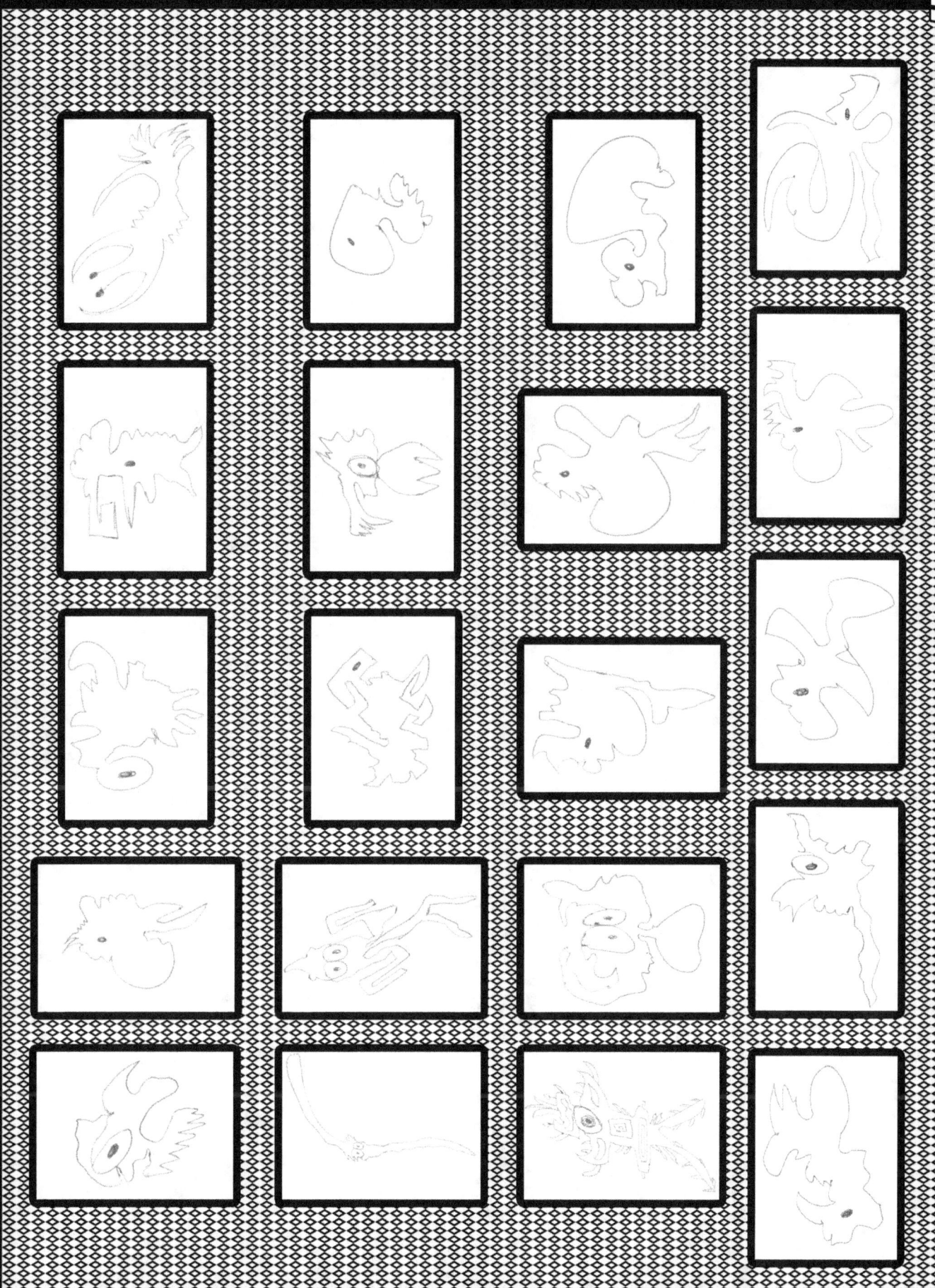

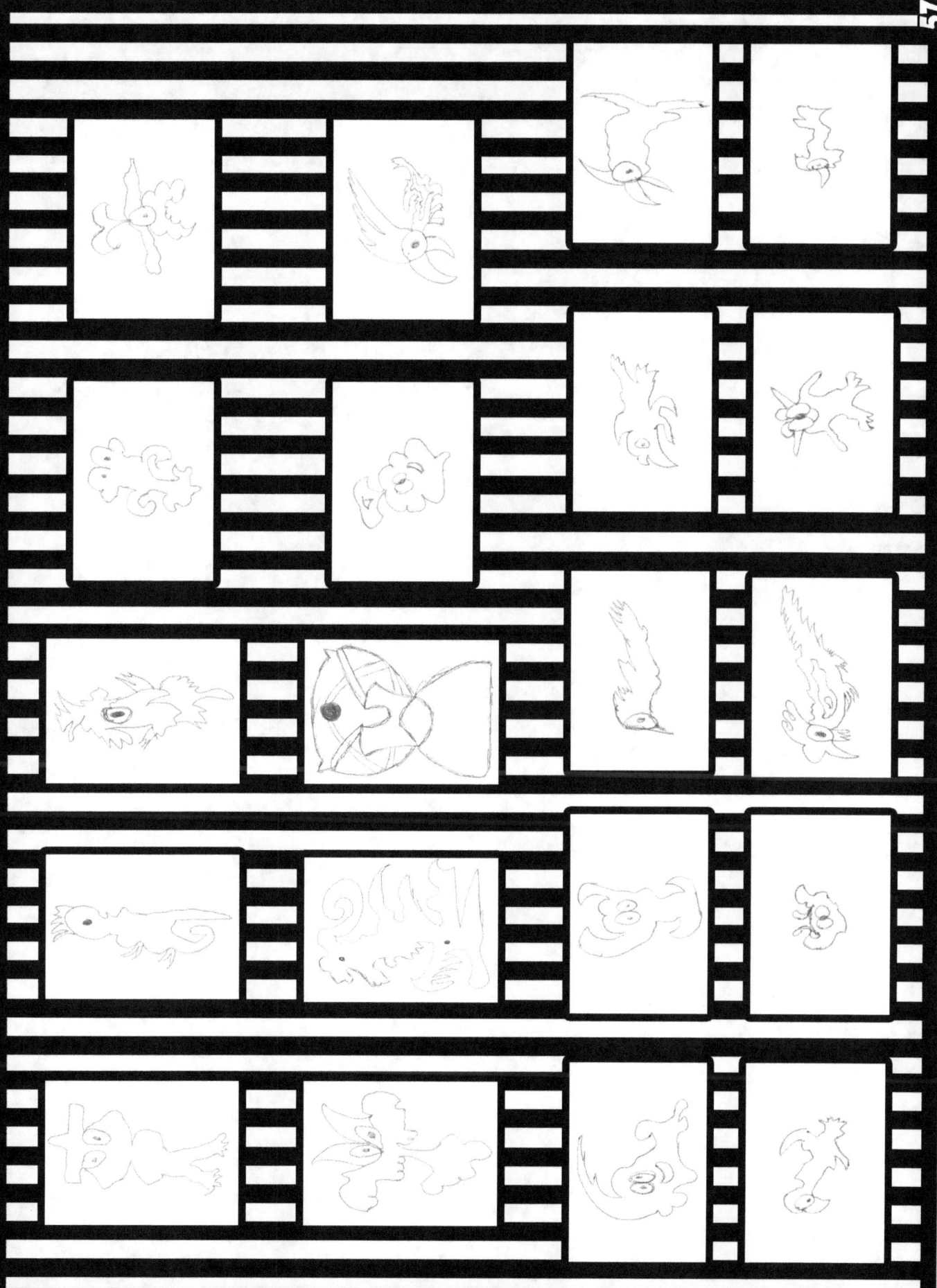

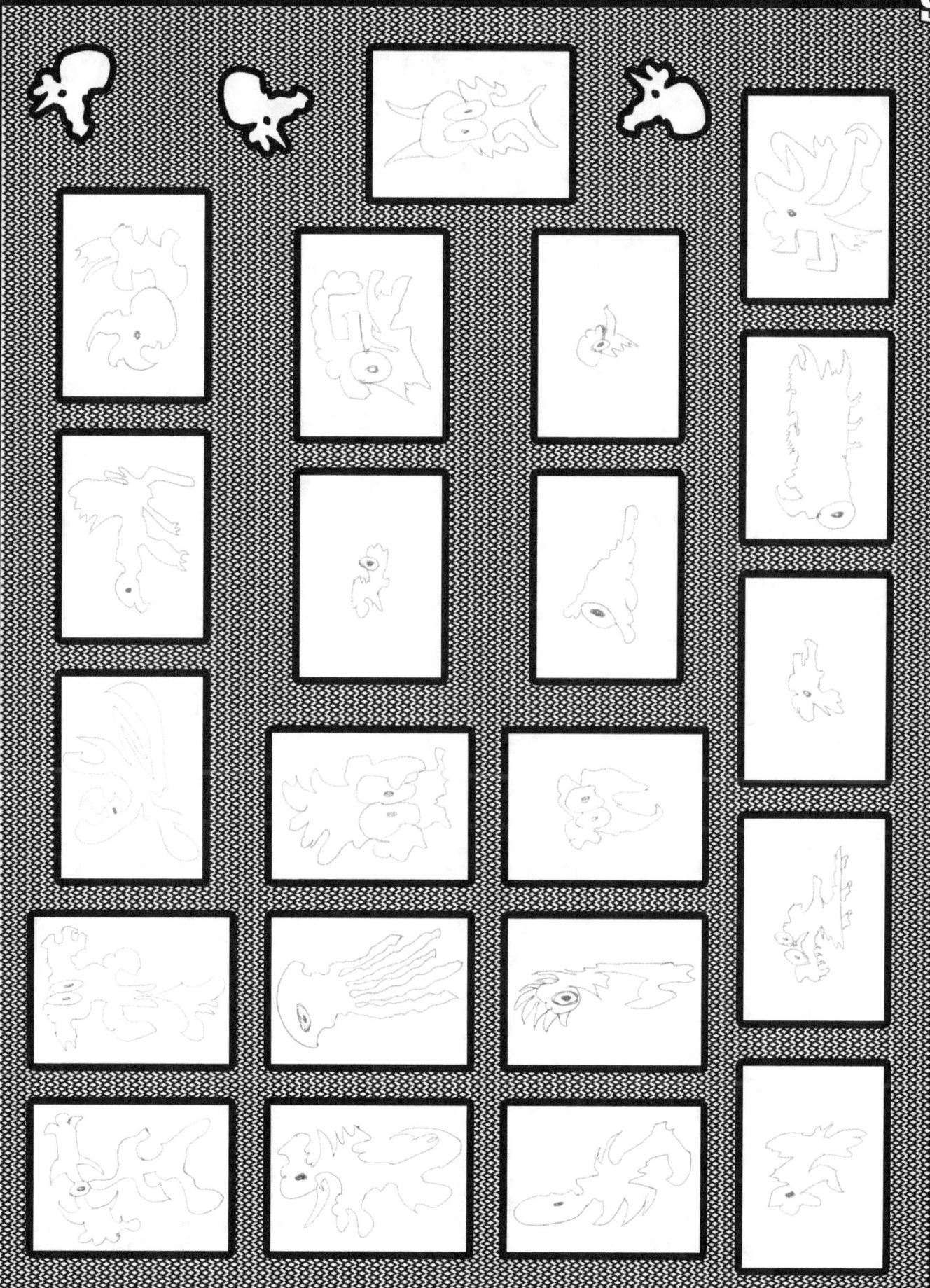

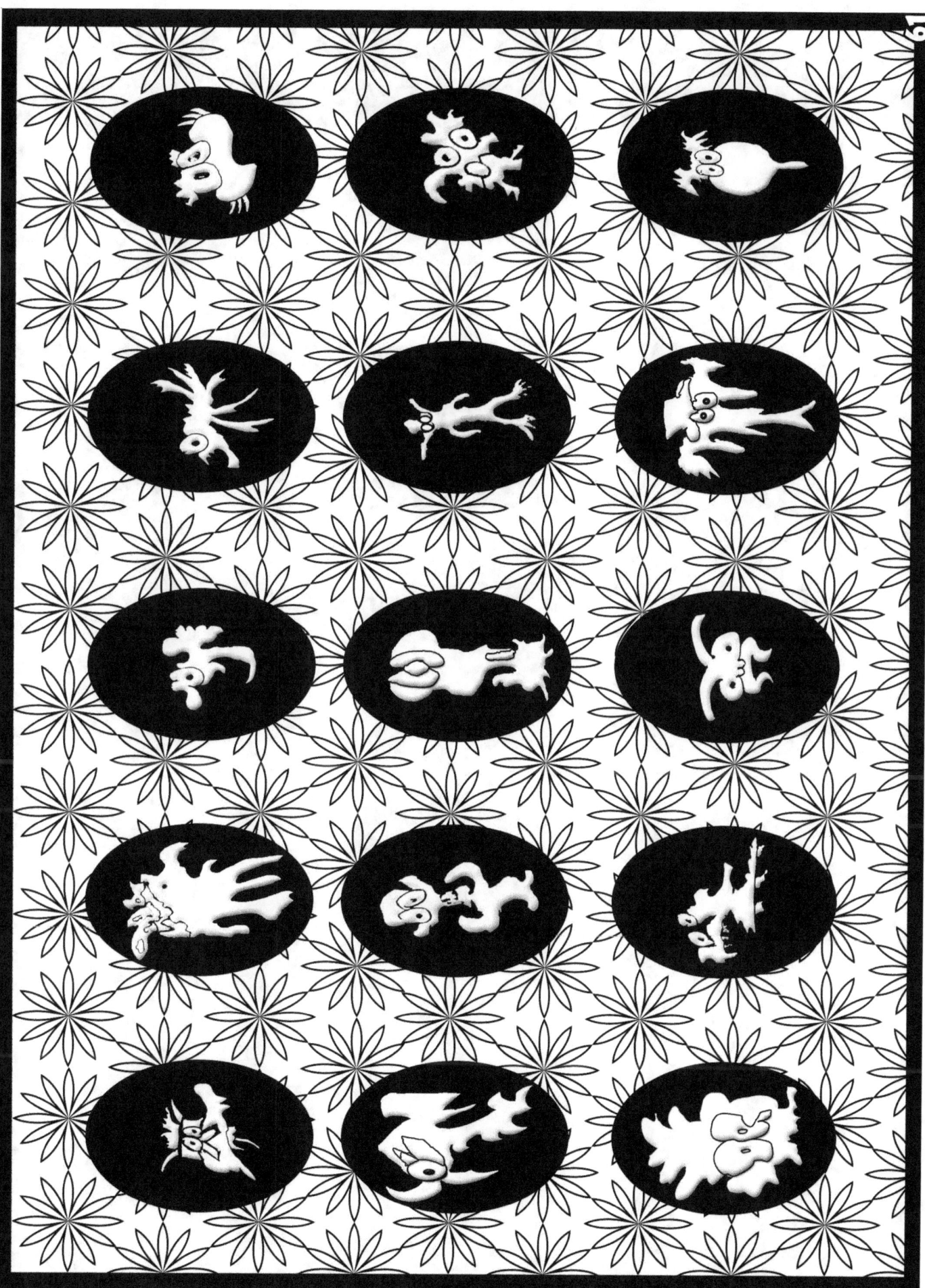

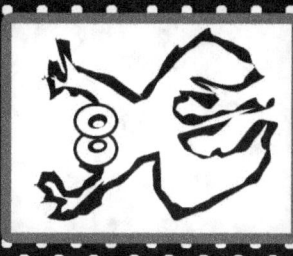
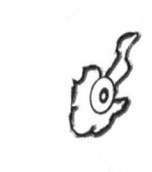
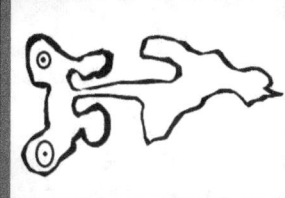
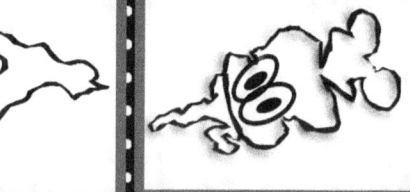
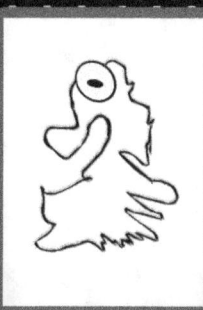
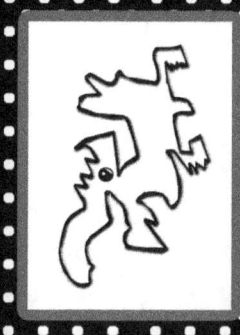
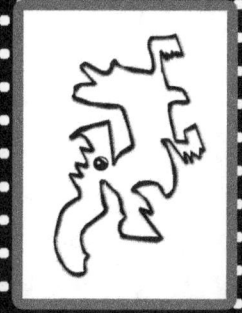
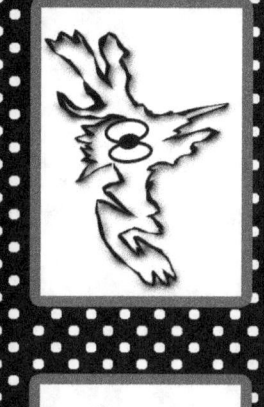
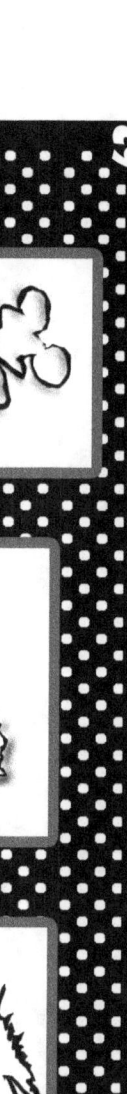
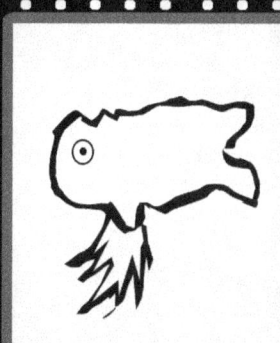
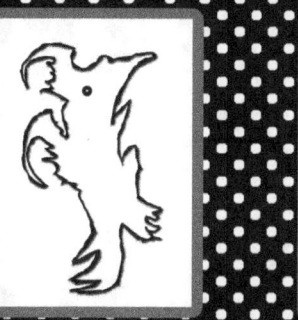
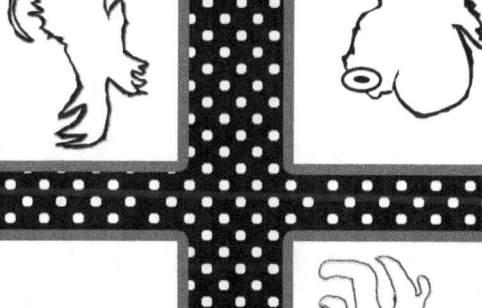
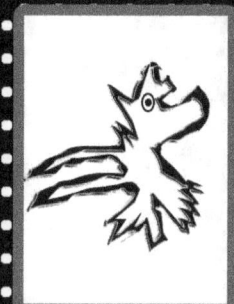
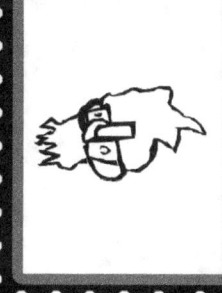
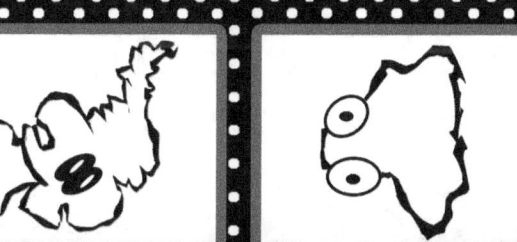
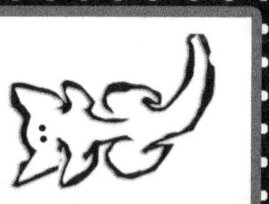
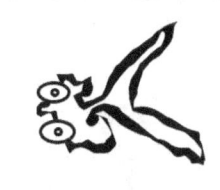

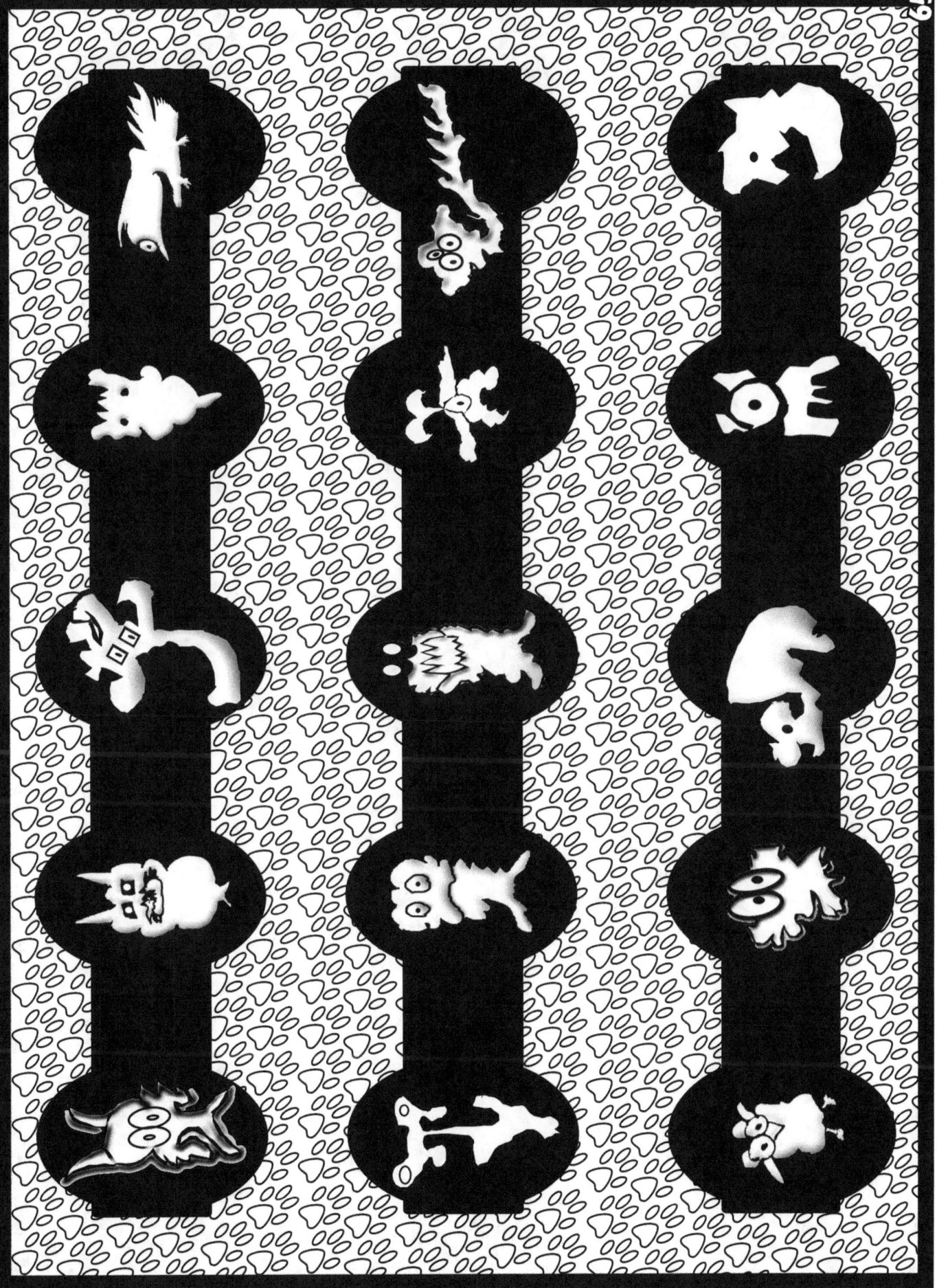

ILLUSTRATIONS

BASKETBALL

1. THE CHARMS COURT
2. FREE THROW LINE
3. THE BATS COURT
4. DEFENCE

BONUS: WRAPPING PAPER

1. AQUARIUM
2. BIRDS
3. STREET
4. WALL
5. FENCE

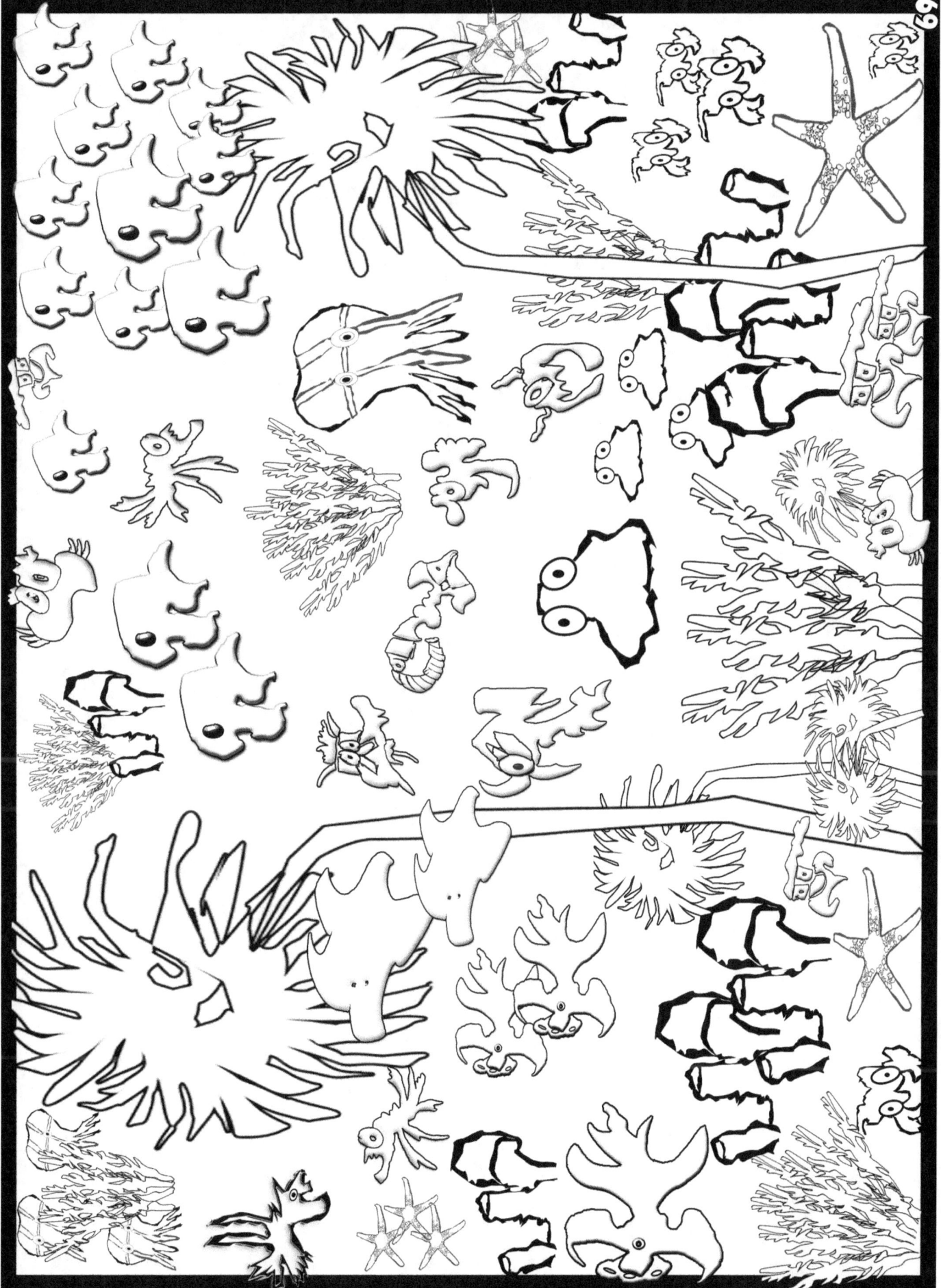

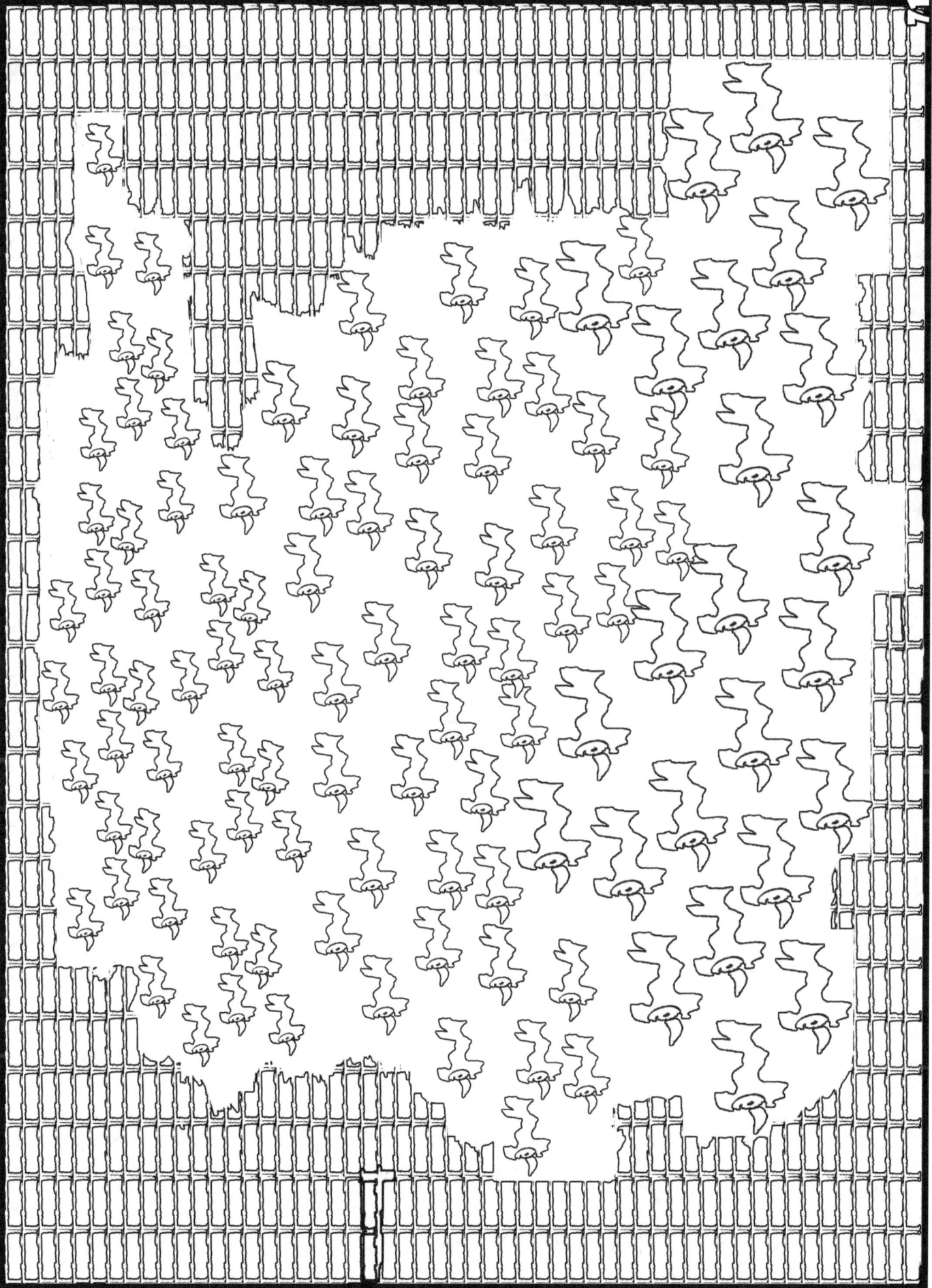

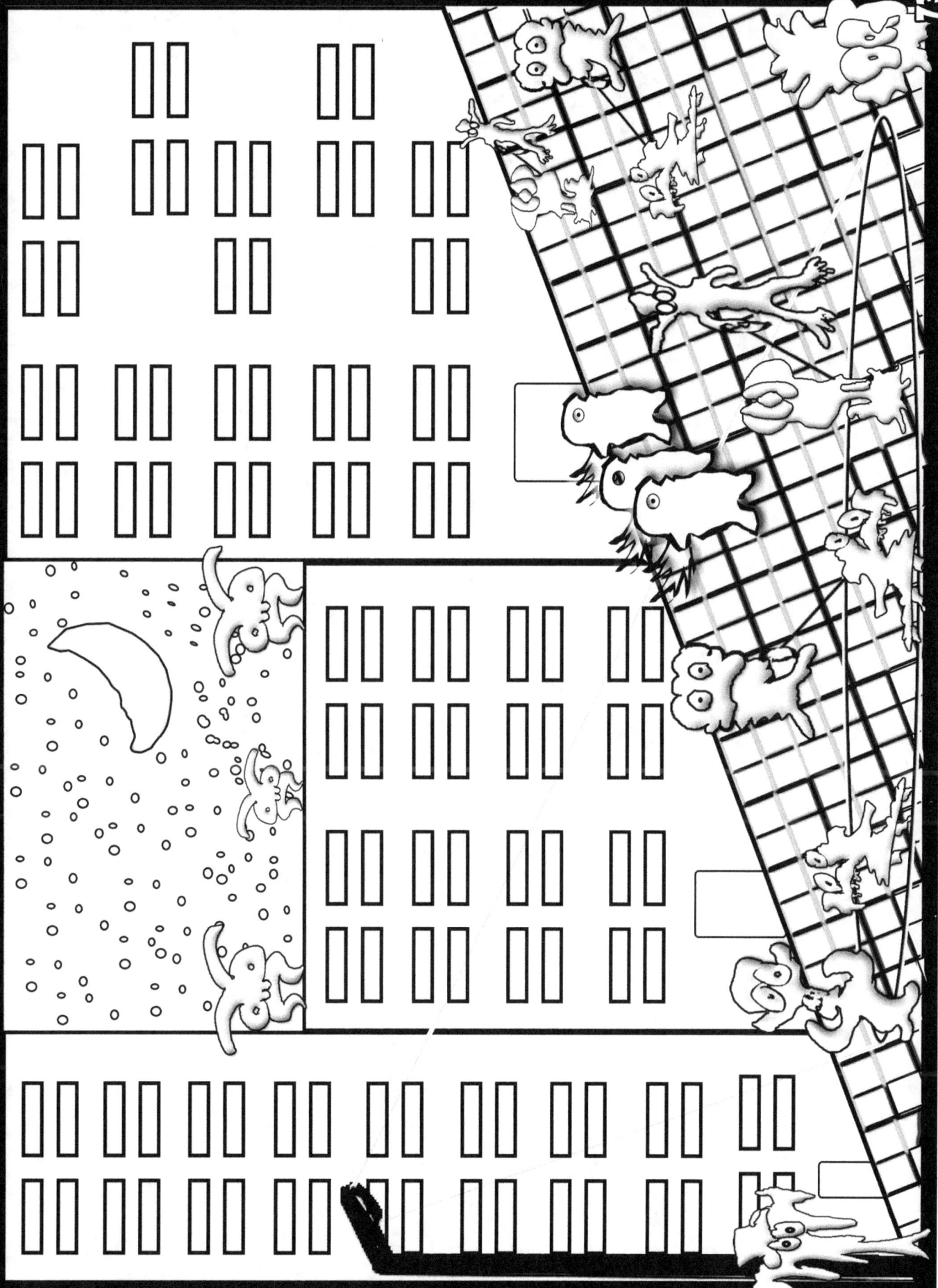

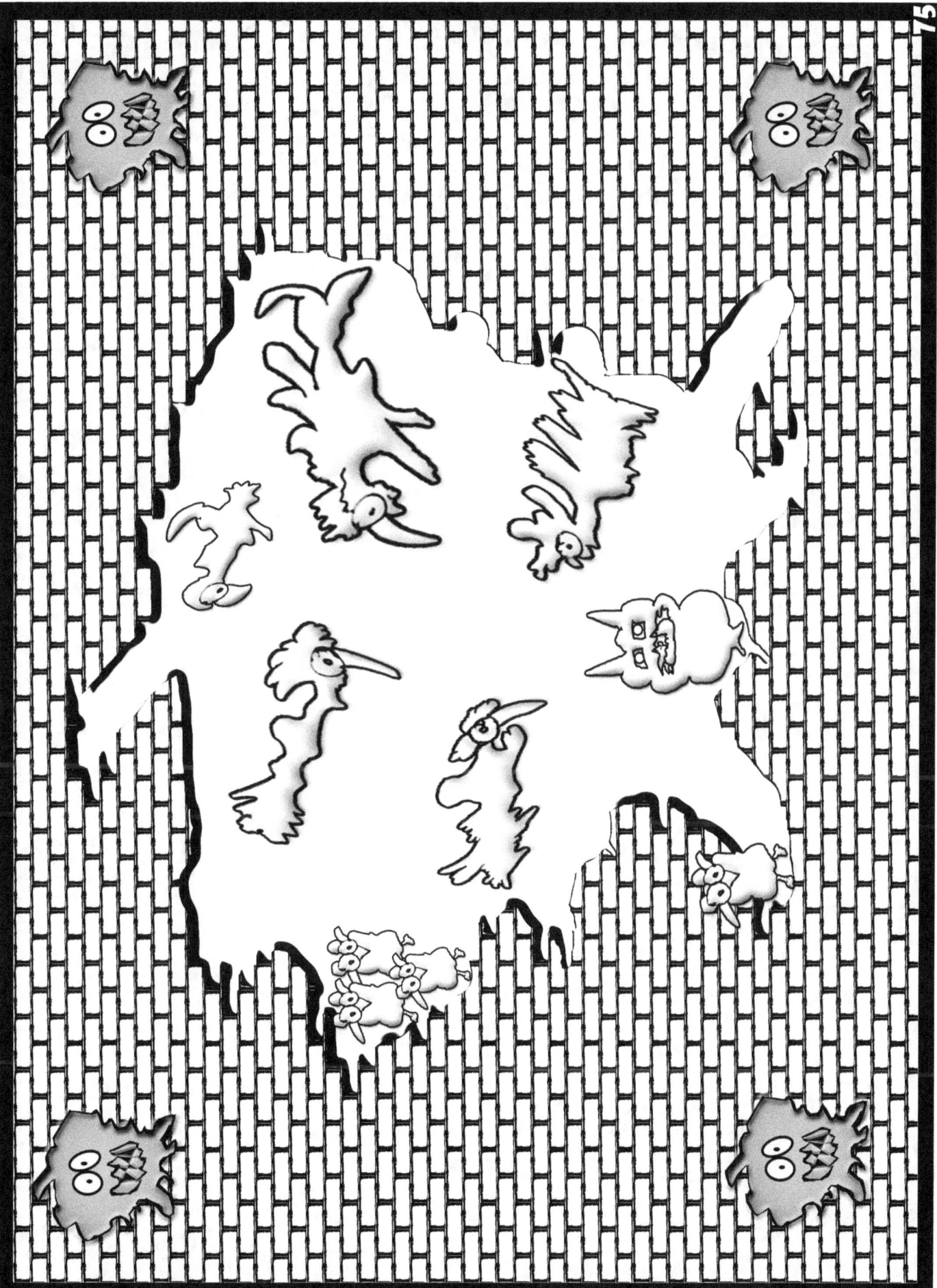

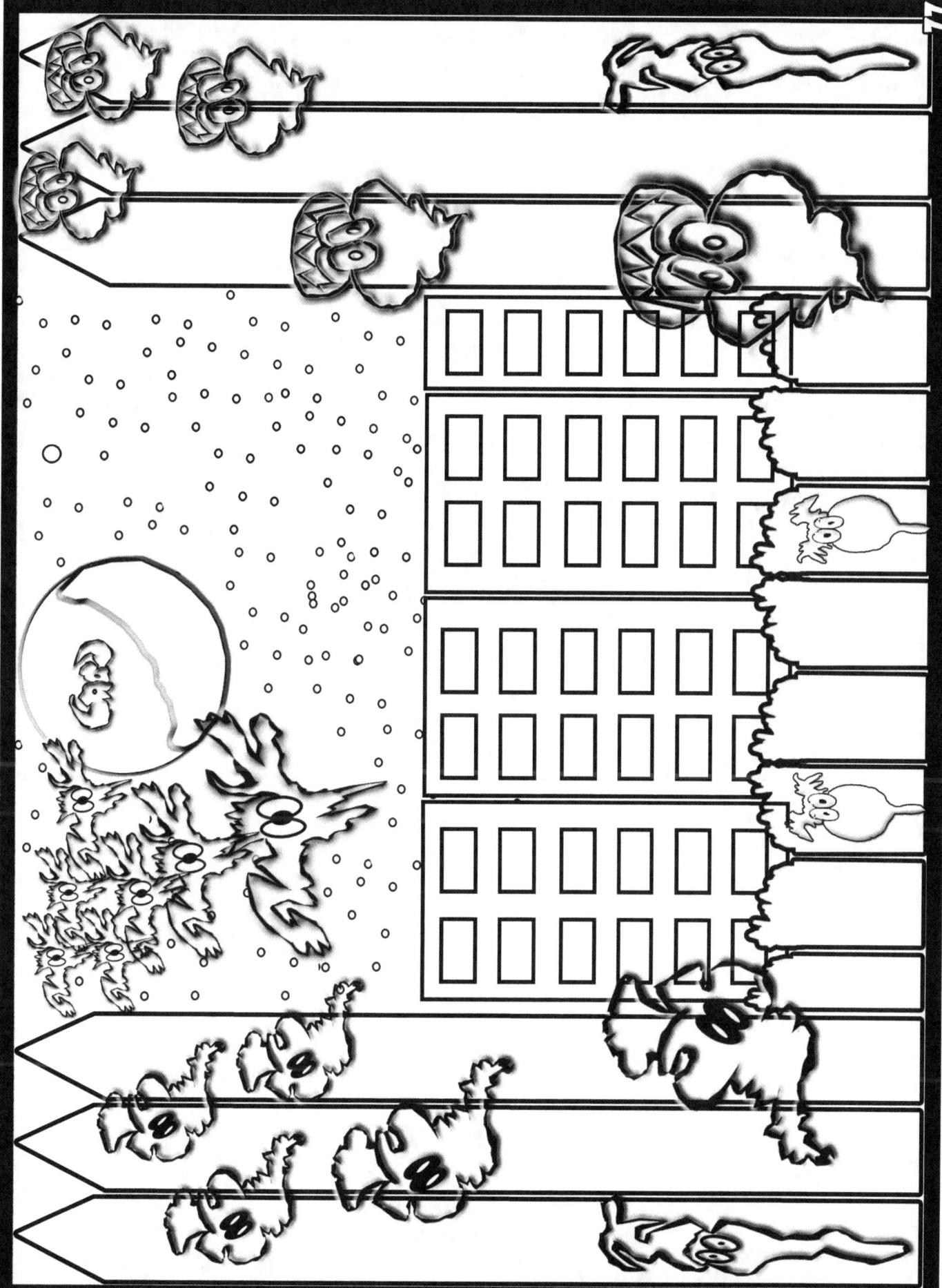

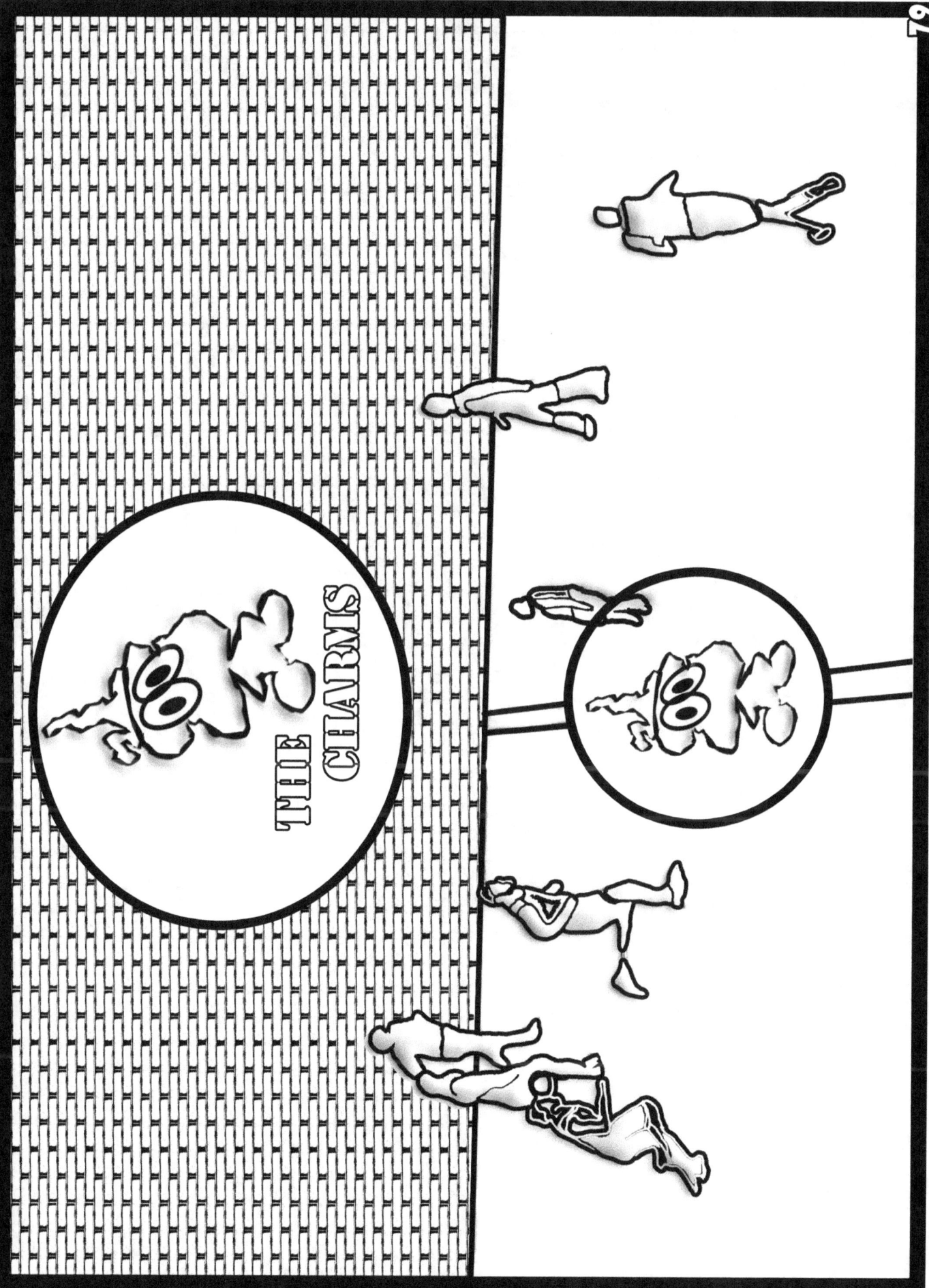

AT THE FREE THROW LINE . . .

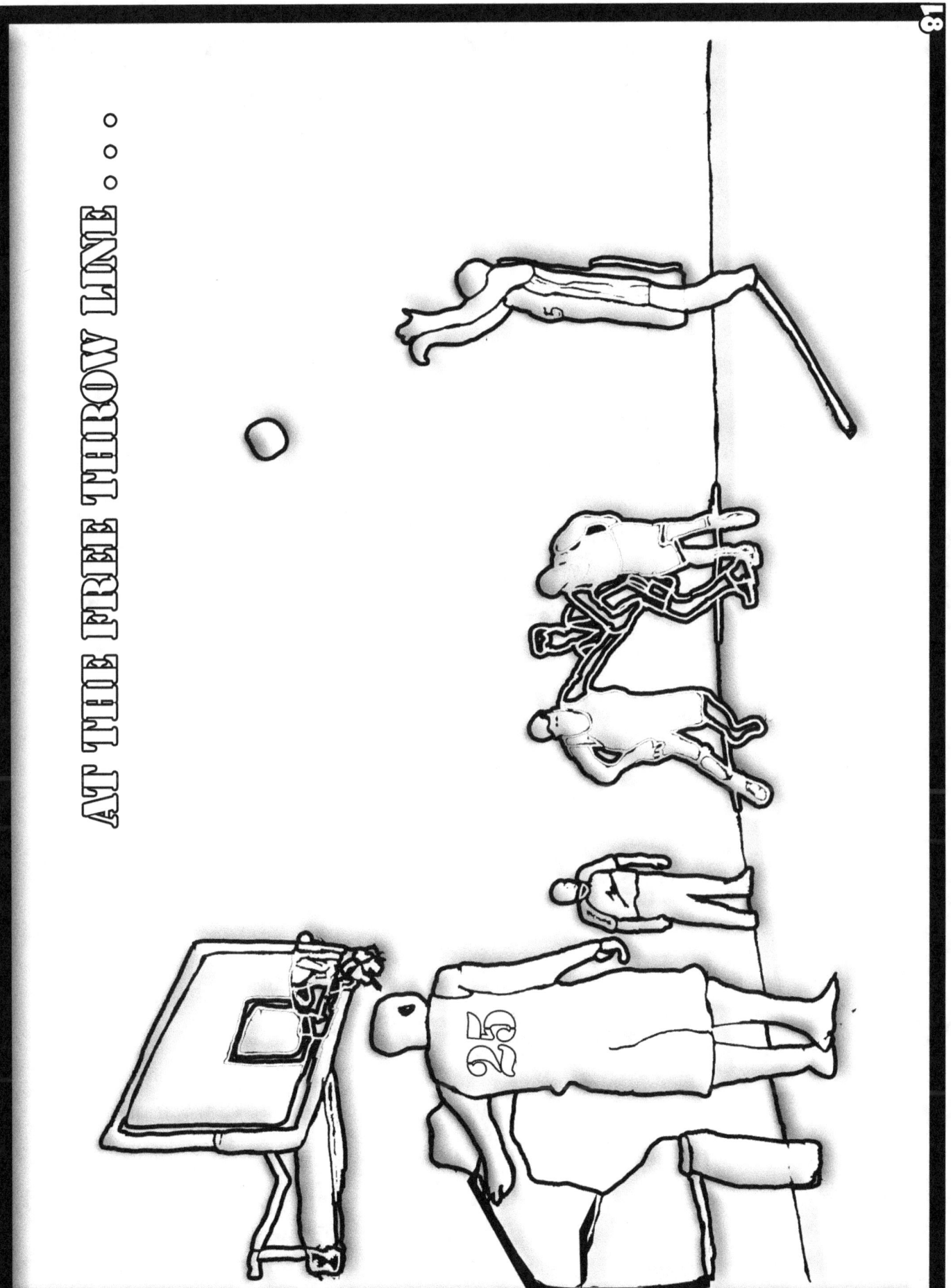

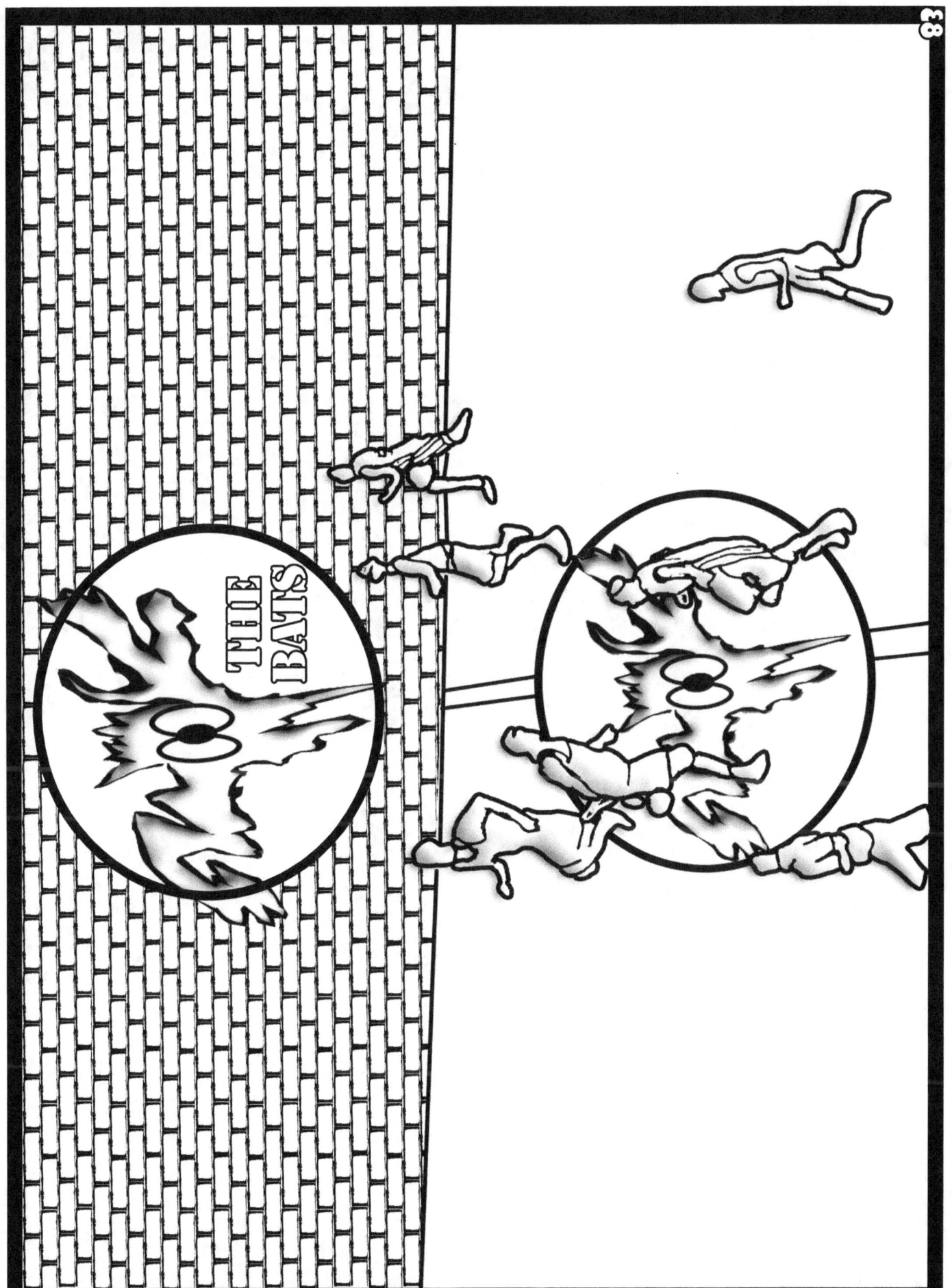

DEFENCE. DEFENCE. DEFENCE.

DEFENCE. DEFENCE. DEFENCE.

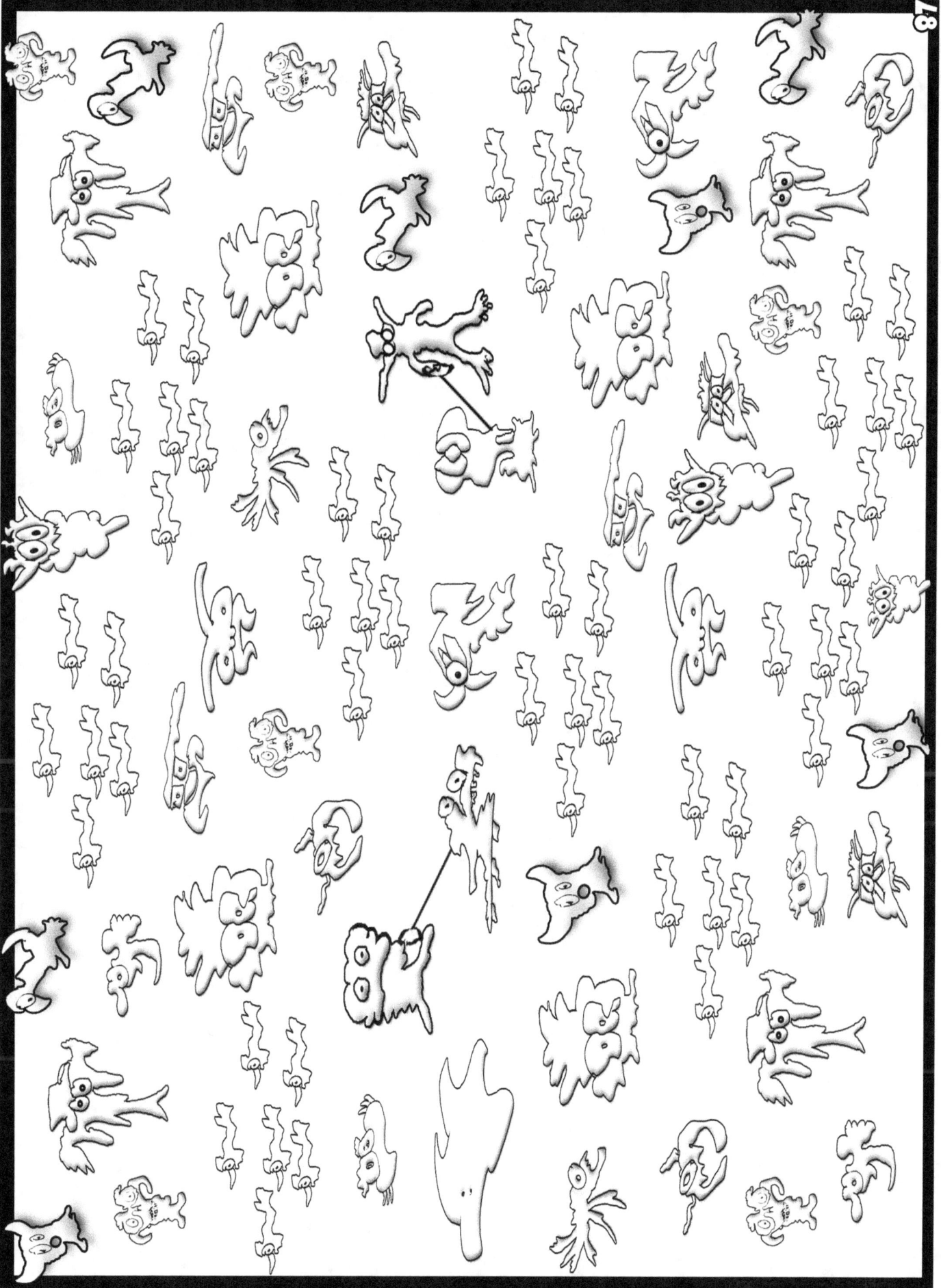

The Just Put An Eye On It! Philosophy

How it Works

Don't think! Just pick up a pen and draw whatever shape comes to mind. To finish it off, Just Put An Eye On It! or two...Everything looks as a fun character if you Just Put An Eye On It!

Why Do It?

If you are feeling tired, bored or your mind just needs a little jolt then taking a few seconds to draw a simple character may be all you need to get back on track. One drawing is all it takes. This simple action can help you regain focus and feel better. Inking and coloring can have the same effect only it will make you feel even better knowing you are bringing to life your very own drawing.

Fun for Everyone

Coloring isn't just for kids. Everyone can take five and let their mind wander for a while. A fun, creative break might be all you need. And parents, don't be scared, go ahead and be one of the kids, even if it is only for five seconds...

DRAW YOU OWN CHARACTERS!

START WITH A SHAPE
THEN PUT AN EYE ON IT!
A SIMPLE DOT WILL DO...

HOW ABOUT STARTING WITH AN EYE?

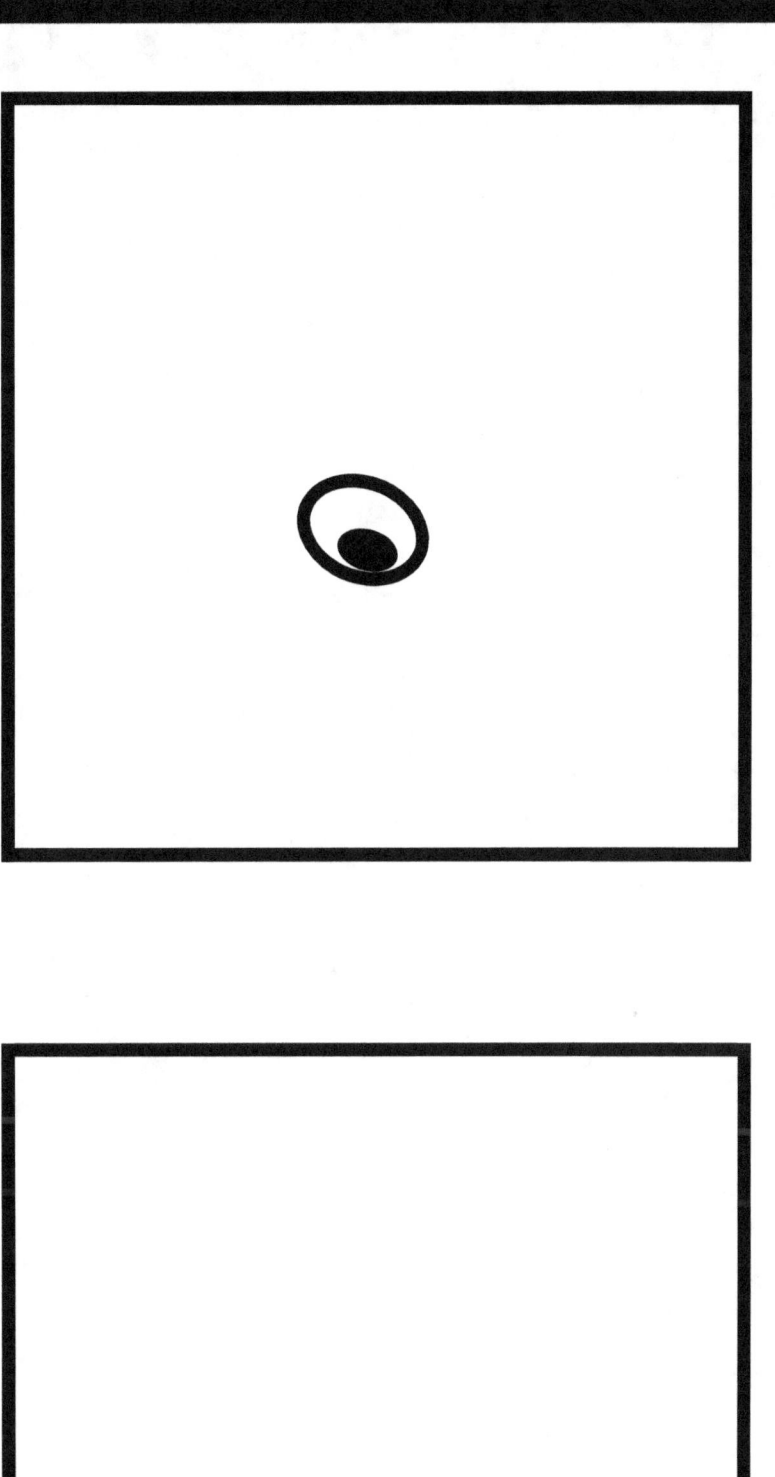

HOW ABOUT STARTING WITH TWO EYES?

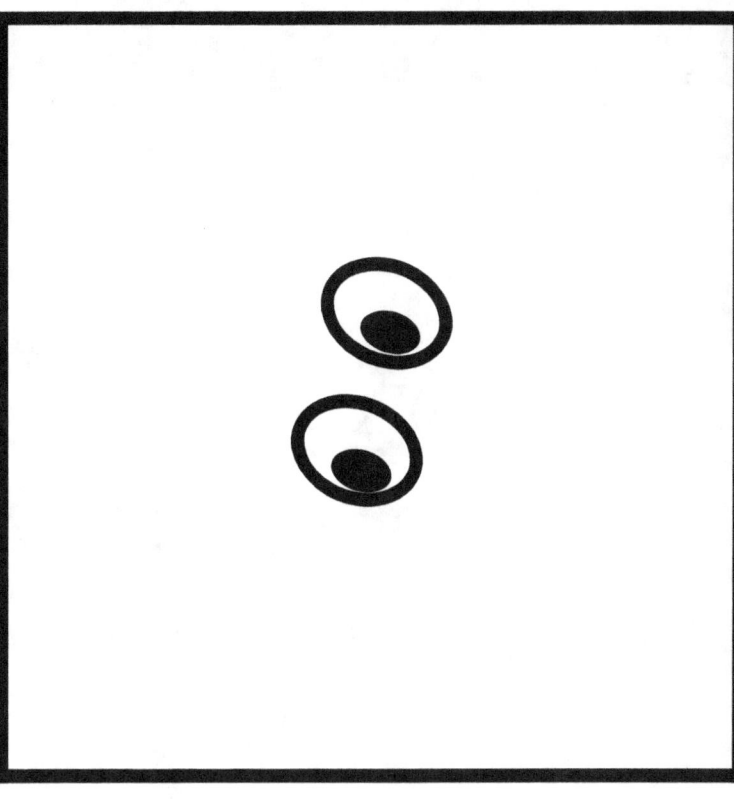

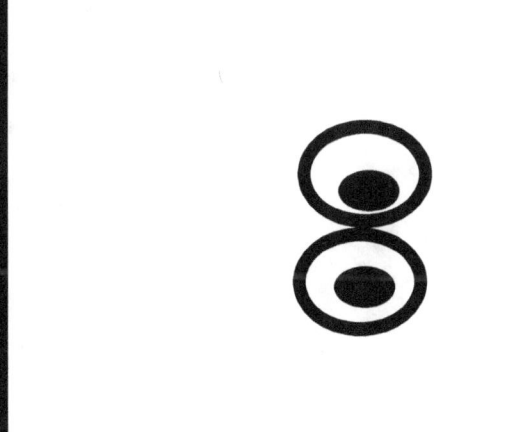

GIVE IT A GO !

AN EYE...
A BEAK...
A SHAPE !

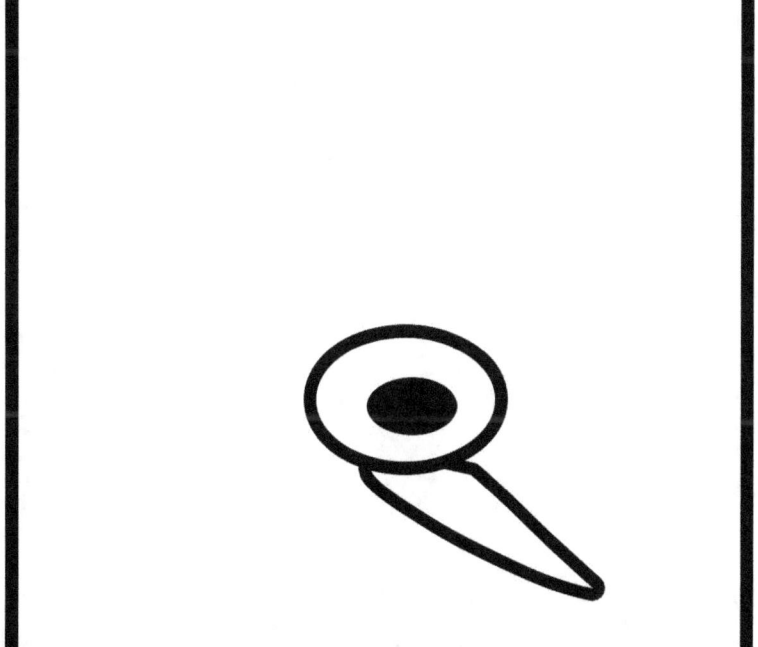

Just Put An Eye On It!

JustPutAnEyeOnIt!

T-SHIRTS

**BAT A.K.A.
THE BATS
T-SHIRT!**

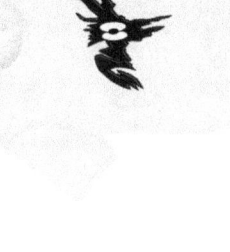

**LUCKY GREEN A.K.A.
THE CHARMS
T-SHIRT!**

**HUG ME IF YOU
CAN BABY GHOST
T-SHIRT!**

HUG ME

IF YOU CAN

www.justputaneyeonit.com

www.ingramcontent.com/pod-product-compliance
Lightning Source LLC
Chambersburg PA
CBHW081547170526
45166CB00009B/2614